Contents

KU-679-234

Revising for Standard Grade Geography

This book is not intended to be a replacement for all of your course notes, but is designed to supplement them and to show you effective ways of answering the questions you will face in the exam. By using this book as you work through the course and prepare for prelims and the national exam, you will consolidate your knowledge and skills and learn how to write good-quality answers which will get you a better grade.

Standard Grade Geography covers a wide range of physical and human topics. It is a very good preparation for Higher and will help to improve your reading, writing, enquiry and map skills as well as your general knowledge of the world around you. By studying Geography, you will improve your understanding of the environment, how it affects us and how we can affect it.

The Standard Grade Geography course is split into seventeen **Key Ideas**. Key Ideas 1 to 6 deal mainly with the physical (natural) environment, Key Ideas 7 to 11 deal with the human environment, and Key Ideas 12 to 17 involve the study of international issues. This sequence from 1 to 17 is significant, as, when you sit the exam, the questions are usually arranged roughly in the same order as the Key Ideas.

How to use this book

The Contents page shows you the order in which the Key Ideas appear. At the beginning of each chapter, you can see the Key Ideas which that particular chapter covers. Within each chapter, there are sections which contain brief summaries of what you should know about the topics in that part of the course.

Important words are highlighted, and you can check the meaning of these by looking them up in the glossary at the end of the book. Each section continues with examples of General and Credit questions, mostly from previous SQA question papers, with sample answers for each.

In each sample answer, you can see how it would be marked and where exactly marks are given. There is also a commentary following each sample answer, giving general advice about that particular question and answer. In this way, you should be able to build up a clear picture of how to write good answers at Standard Grade.

General tips about writing good exam answers

The first thing you should do when answering an exam question is to look at the number of marks allocated to it. Use this as a guide to how much you should write. If it is a six-mark question at Credit, you should write a good bit more than you would for a four-mark one.

Try to develop your answers into good explanations. Consider these responses from two different pupils:

Pupil 1. 'This is a good site for a factory because it is next to a main road, giving it easy access.'
Pupil 2. 'This is a good site for a factory because it is next to a main road, giving it easy access and allowing lorries to transport goods in and out quickly.'

The second pupil has developed the initial statement into a more detailed response and gains two marks instead of one.

There are two **elements** in Standard Grade Geography. Exam questions are either **Knowledge and Understanding (KU)** or **Enquiry Skills (ES)**. In KU questions, you will be expected to demonstrate good geographical knowledge which you will learn throughout the course. In ES questions, you will be expected to evaluate the resources shown in diagrams you are given. Don't be put off if these diagrams are about something you haven't studied. You will have learned how to interpret unfamiliar resources and should still be able to write a good answer.

Look out for questions which ask you to **explain**. In answering these, you must give reasons for the points which you are making. This means that you will be using phrases such as 'because' and 'due to'. It is vital that you do this – otherwise you will lose a lot of marks.

Some questions ask you whether or not you agree with a statement. Make it clear at the beginning whether you agree or disagree. Start by saying 'I agree/disagree because …', before going on to give your reasons for doing

BrightRED Results

Standard Grade
GEOGRAPHY

Ralph Harnden

First published in 2010 by:
Bright Red Publishing Ltd
6 Stafford Street
Edinburgh
EH3 7AU

A CIP record for this book is available from the British Library

ISBN 978-1-906736-10-1

With thanks to:
PDQ Digital Media Solutions (layout) and Ivor Normand (copy-edit)

Cover design by Caleb Rutherford – e i d e t i c

Illustrations by PDQ Digital Media Solutions

Every effort has been made to seek all copyright holders. If any have been overlooked then Bright Red Publishing will be delighted to make the necessary arrangements.

Acknowledgements
Ordnance Survey © Crown Copyright. All rights reserved. Licence number 100049324 (pages 81, 85 & 89);
Photograph © Toyota (GB) PLC (page 45);

Bright Red Publishing would also like to thank the Scottish Qualifications Authority for use of Past Exam Questions. Answers do not emanate from the SQA.

Printed and bound in Scotland by Scotprint

so. It is OK to say that you only partly agree with a statement, remembering to give your reasons, before going on to say that you partly disagree, again giving your reasons.

If you are asked a question about **gathering techniques**, you will be expected to write about ways in which information about a particular area or investigation can be collected. Be precise in your answer. Make sure that you specify to whom you will be sending a questionnaire or whom you will be interviewing. You must also explain why the methods you have chosen are useful.

In **processing techniques** questions, you must choose appropriate ways to display information which you are given. For example, if you are given a list of land use data in a table which is already in percentages, it would be simple to show this in the form of a pie chart. You will also have to explain why the methods you have chosen are suitable. In this case, a pie chart would be appropriate because the data is already in percentages. You will be expected to give a different reason for each technique, so avoid giving the same reason twice.

The last chapter of this book features a section on answering Ordnance Survey map questions. The map question is worth about one third of the marks, so spend about a third of the time on it. For example, on the General paper, you might spend about 25 minutes on the map question, while on the Credit paper you may need up to 40 minutes. You should make sure you get lots of practice at answering map questions, as they are such a major part of every exam.

If you are not sure about the meaning of map symbols, you can look at the key printed on the map extracts – but it is worth learning what the main symbols mean, as this will save you time in the exam. Good map answers will refer directly to named features on the map and should usually include some grid references. Make sure that you can do grid references accurately – **eastings** before **northings**, or along the corridor and then up the stairs!

Finally, careful revision before your prelim and your exam will be particularly important in helping you to achieve a good grade, as all of the award in Standard Grade Geography depends on your exam performance. There is no coursework element as there is in some other subjects. The purpose of this book is to help you to do well in your exam. The following list gives you some ideas of what you should do during the exam.

Look out for

Sample answers to questions on gathering techniques and on processing techniques are given throughout this book.

Tips to follow during the exam

1. Write in pen. Pencil can be hard to read.
2. Read the instructions on the front of the paper carefully.
3. In the **General** exam, you write on the question paper. In the **Credit** exam, you write in a separate answer booklet.
4. Make sure you know when the exam finishes. The General paper lasts for 1 hour and 25 minutes, the Credit paper for 2 hours.
5. Read the questions carefully and study the resources which go with them. They are there to give you prompts to help you with your answer. Use your knowledge too!
6. Look at the number of marks for each question. Write more for a question worth six marks than for one worth three or four marks.
7. **'Explain'** questions mean that you must give reasons for your answer.
8. Avoid writing lists. You are expected to write in sentences.
9. Give grid references when you are referring to places on the OS map (six figures where appropriate).
10. In the Credit paper, leave a gap after each question so that you can add to it later if you have time.
11. Keep an eye on the time, and make sure you leave enough time to finish the paper.
12. If you have any time left at the end of the exam, use it **productively** by trying to add more to your answers.
13. Keep your writing legible. If the examiner reading your answers can't read it, you won't get the marks you deserve!
14. Keep a cool head. Don't panic!

KEY IDEA 1

Physical landscapes are the product of natural processes and are always changing.

This Key Idea specifies that you need to know about the processes which shape the landscape. In particular, learn about glaciated areas and rivers and their valleys. To be able to explain the formation of different landscape features, you should study **weathering**, **erosion**, **transportation** and **deposition**.

Glaciation

What you should know at **General** **and** **Credit** **level …**

When the last ice age finished more than 10 000 years ago, a variety of different landscapes were left behind by the ice sheets and the meltwater flowing from them. This created landscapes of **glacial erosion** and landscapes of **glacial deposition**. Exam questions will expect you to be able to identify glacial landscape features and to explain how they are formed. To do this, you must be able to refer to processes of weathering and glacial erosion. These are **frost shattering**, **abrasion** and **ice plucking**.

This answer shows a good understanding of the processes involved in the formation of a terminal moraine. It conveys the idea that, as the ice moved forward, material was carried by the ice until the glacier melted. The diagrams show the stages in the formation of a terminal moraine, and the labels explain each stage well. At General level, these diagrams would achieve full marks on their own.

General question 1

Explain how a terminal moraine is formed. You may wish to use one or more diagrams to illustrate your answer.

(3 KU marks)

General answer 1

As the ice sheet moved forward, it bulldozed a large mound of rocks and boulders in front of it (✓). This is called moraine (✓). When the ice stopped moving forward and began to melt, the moraine was left behind, marking the furthest point which the ice had reached (✓). This ridge of material is called a terminal moraine (✓).

Diagram 1: <u>Formation of terminal moraine</u>

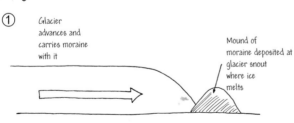

① Glacier advances and carries moraine with it

Mound of moraine deposited at glacier snout where ice melts

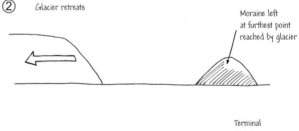

② Glacier retreats

Moraine left at furthest point reached by glacier

③ After the ice age

Terminal Moraine

General question 2

Explain how an arête is formed. You may use one or more diagrams to illustrate your answer.

(3 KU marks)

General answer 2

An arête is formed when two corries are formed next to each other on a mountain (✓). As the corries are made deeper by glacial erosion, a ridge of land is left between them (✓). This ridge is made sharp and jagged by frost shattering (✓). This is where water gets into cracks in the rock, expanding when it freezes and breaking them apart (✓).

Diagram 2: Formation of an arête

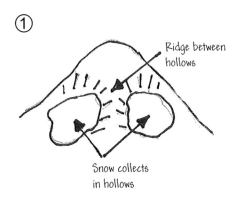

①

Ridge between hollows

Snow collects in hollows

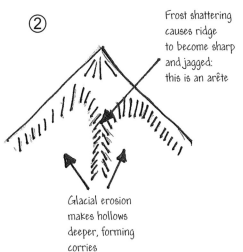

②

Frost shattering causes ridge to become sharp and jagged: this is an arête

Glacial erosion makes hollows deeper, forming corries

This is a very good answer at General level. There is a good explanation of how frost shattering creates a sharp ridge in between the corries, and the diagrams show how the shape of the mountain changes due to glaciation. This answer easily scores full marks and would get at least two marks for the well-labelled diagrams on their own.

Look out for

When answering questions about the formation of landscape features, it is good practice to include a series of simple diagrams to illustrate the processes at work. If your diagrams are accurately labelled, you will gain extra marks.

Credit question 1

Explain how a U-shaped valley is formed. You may use one or more diagrams to illustrate your answer.

(4 KU marks)

Credit answer 1

A U-shaped valley is formed when a glacier flows along an existing V-shaped valley (✔). As it does so, it deepens and widens the valley due to erosion (✔). At the bottom of the glacier, there are large chunks of rock which are frozen into its base, and they scrape away at the valley bottom. This is abrasion (✔). Also, the glacier ice may freeze onto loosened rocks on the valley bottom and slowly pull them out. This is called ice plucking (✔). The valley is also attacked above and below the glacier by the process of frost shattering (✔), which happens when water gets into cracks within the rock and freezes, expanding as it does so (✔). This slowly causes the rock to break up. As a result of all of these processes, the valley is made much larger and more U-shaped (✔). The stream which is left in the bottom is too small to have carved such a valley on its own, so is known as a misfit stream (✔).

Diagram 3: <u>Formation of a U-shaped valley</u>

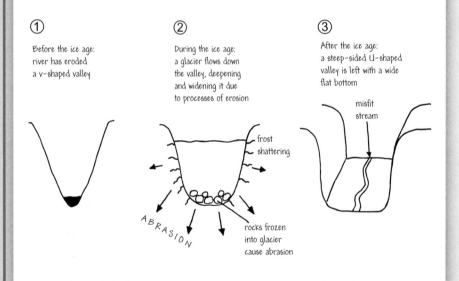

① Before the ice age: river has eroded a v-shaped valley

② During the ice age: a glacier flows down the valley, deepening and widening it due to processes of erosion

③ After the ice age: a steep-sided U-shaped valley is left with a wide flat bottom

frost shattering

ABRASION

rocks frozen into glacier cause abrasion

misfit stream

This is a very detailed answer which shows a good understanding of all the processes of glacial erosion. Rather than just listing each process, the candidate has explained each one in relation to the formation of a U-shaped valley. The candidate's diagrams show good progression from a V-shaped valley at the start to the finished U-shaped valley. The diagrams are made better by the addition of explanatory labels. These diagrams on their own could achieve full marks.

Look out for

Make sure you write your Us and Vs clearly! If you are writing about glaciated landscapes, and the way you have written your U makes it look like a V-shaped valley, you may lose a mark. Remember that glaciated valleys are U-shaped, river valleys are V-shaped!

Credit question 2

Explain the formation of a corrie.

(4 KU marks)

Credit answer 2

Snow accumulates in a hollow on the north-facing slope of a mountain (✓). As more snow falls, the layers at the bottom turn to ice, and a glacier is formed when the ice starts to grow slowly downhill due to gravity (✓). The glacier erodes the hollow, making it larger (✓) by processes such as abrasion, ice plucking and frost shattering (✓). Abrasion happens when rocks frozen into the base of the glacier act like sandpaper and scrape away at the base of the hollow (✓). Sometimes ice freezes onto rocks which have been loosened by frost shattering and pulls them out as the ice moves downhill. This is ice plucking (✓). After the ice age, a large bowl-shaped hollow is left which might contain a small loch known as a corrie lochan or tarn (✓).

This answer easily gets full marks, as the candidate shows an excellent understanding of how a corrie is formed. It explains how the process begins with the formation of a glacier and then how the glacier carves into the hollow to turn it into a corrie. It also contains good explanations of how glacial processes such as abrasion and ice plucking are involved. The candidate includes a good series of diagrams which, crucially, have detailed explanatory labels.

Diagram 4: Corrie formation

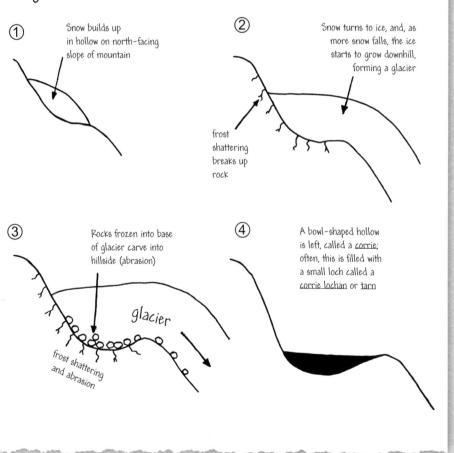

① Snow builds up in hollow on north-facing slope of mountain

② Snow turns to ice, and, as more snow falls, the ice starts to grow downhill, forming a glacier

frost shattering breaks up rock

③ Rocks frozen into base of glacier carve into hillside (abrasion)

glacier

frost shattering and abrasion

④ A bowl-shaped hollow is left, called a corrie; often, this is filled with a small loch called a corrie lochan or tarn

Look out for

To answer questions about glacial landforms well, you will need to know the meaning of key words such as **moraine**, **boulder clay**, **outwash plain**, **corrie**, **arête**, **pyramidal peak**, **U-shaped valley**, **hanging valley** and **truncated spur**. Your answers should refer to processes such as **frost shattering**, **plucking** and **abrasion** and also contain explanations of how these work. A good answer often contains a series of diagrams, which must have explanatory labels.

Rivers and their valleys

What you should know at  level ...

There are questions about rivers almost every year. You should be able to identify different river features such as **tributaries**, **meanders**, **flood plains** and **oxbow lakes** and also what the characteristics of river valleys are in their upper, middle and lower courses. You must also be able to explain how river landforms such as a **V-shaped valley** and an oxbow lake are formed. Knowledge of processes such as **weathering**, **corrasion** and **hydraulic action** will help you to give first-class answers.

Credit question 1

Explain how a V-shaped river valley is formed. You may use one or more diagrams to illustrate your answer.

(4 KU marks)

Credit answer 1

As the river flows downhill, it moves fast and can carry along large stones which scrape away at the bed and banks of the river (✓). This deepens the valley and is called corrasion (✓). On the slopes above the river, weathering processes such as frost shattering take place (✓). Water gets into cracks in the rock, expands when it turns to ice and breaks the rock apart when this happens repeatedly (✓). This material then moves downhill into the river, due to gravity or rain washing it away (✓), where it is then carried downstream and used by the river to carry out more corrasion (✓).

Although this response does not include diagrams, the answer still gets full marks because it shows a good knowledge of both the processes of river erosion and of weathering on the valley sides. It contains explanations both of corrasion and of frost shattering and how these help to form the V-shaped valley.

Credit question 2

Explain how an oxbow lake is formed. You may use one or more diagrams to illustrate your answer.

(4 KU marks)

Look out for

Questions about physical landscapes are often tested using Ordnance Survey map extracts. See Chapter 10 for advice on answering map questions about glaciated scenery and rivers.

Credit answer 2

On the outside bend of a meander, where the current flows fastest, the river cuts into the bank of the river (✓), eroding it away and creating a river cliff (✓). Where two meanders are close together, they are eroded away until they are so close together that the river eventually breaks through the neck (✓) and creates a new straighter course for itself (✓). The old meander loop is left behind and is eventually sealed off by deposition from the river (✓), creating an abandoned meander known as an oxbow lake (✓).

This answer is well expressed because it shows good understanding of the different stages over which an oxbow lake is formed. Although it does not refer to specific erosion processes by name (such as corrasion), it gives good explanations of how the erosion happened and uses appropriate geographical terms such as river cliff and meander neck. The series of diagrams clearly shows the different stages of oxbow lake formation and has detailed explanatory labels. Both the written answer and the diagrams could achieve full marks separately.

Diagram 5: <u>Formation of an oxbow lake</u>

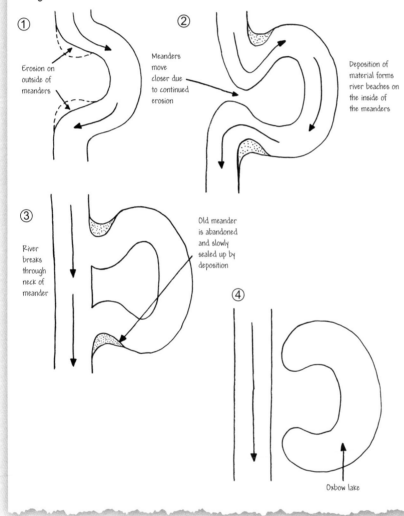

① Erosion on outside of meanders

Meanders move closer due to continued erosion

② Deposition of material forms river beaches on the inside of the meanders

③ River breaks through neck of meander

Old meander is abandoned and slowly sealed up by deposition

④

Oxbow lake

Look out for

To give good answers to river questions, you will need to know how rivers erode their courses and when they deposit material. You should be able to explain the formation of features such as **V-shaped valleys**, **waterfalls**, **oxbow lakes** and river **deltas**. It is well worth learning how to draw diagrams of features such as oxbow lakes to enhance your answer.

KEY IDEA 2

The elements of weather can be identified, observed, measured, recorded and classified. As a result, dynamic patterns can be identified and used for forecasting.

This Key Idea specifies that you need to know how weather information is collected; the names of weather instruments; the weather elements they measure and the units these are measured in. You should also be able to interpret various types of weather map, including **synoptic charts** used by the Meteorological Office. To do this, you should know about **air masses**, fronts, pressure systems and synoptic (weather) symbols.

Measuring the weather

What you should know at **General** **level ...**

You must learn the names of the weather elements, the name of the instrument which gathers information about each one and the units it is measured in. You should also be able to recognise a picture of each weather instrument and assess the suitability of various locations for the siting of a weather station. It is also worth remembering that a **Stevenson Screen** is a specially designed box containing maximum and minimum thermometers. The following table shows information about the weather elements which are most likely to appear in the question papers.

Weather element	*Units of measurement*	*Weather instrument*
temperature	degrees Centigrade	maximum–minimum thermometer
sunshine	hours	sunshine recorder
precipitation	millimetres	rain gauge
wind speed	kilometres/miles per hour	anemometer
wind direction	points of the compass	wind vane
air pressure	millibars	barometer/barograph
cloud cover	oktas	estimate
visibility	kilometres	

Diagram 6: <u>Weather station instruments</u>

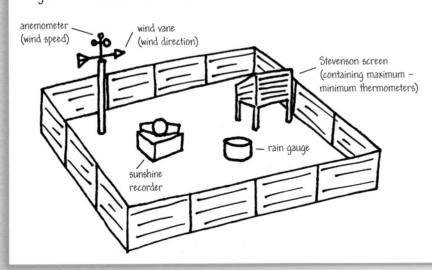

anemometer (wind speed)
wind vane (wind direction)
Stevenson screen (containing maximum – minimum thermometers)
rain gauge
sunshine recorder

Diagram 7: A barograph (measures air pressure)

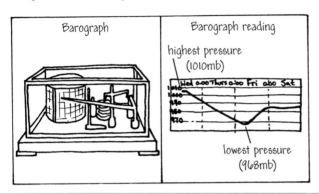

General question 1

Weather Station Sites

Look at the diagram below. Do you agree that site A is the best site for the school weather station? Give reasons for your choice.

(3 KU marks)

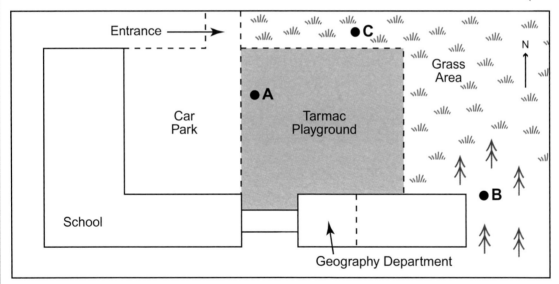

General answer 1

No, site C would be a better location for the weather station, because site A is above tarmac, which would give inaccurate temperature readings (✓), and a weather station here is more likely to be damaged, being located in the playground (✓). Site C would be better because it is above grass, which would reflect less heat, giving more accurate temperature readings (✓), and it is also less sheltered than sites B or C, giving more accurate readings generally (✓).

*Note that, in a 'choice' question such as this, marks can be gained by giving positive reasons for the site you have chosen but also by giving negative reasons for the sites you have rejected. The key point, though, is that you **must** give reasons.*

General question 2

Air Masses affecting Britain

Look at the diagram below.
  (i)   Describe the type of weather Britain might have with air mass D.   **(2 KU marks)**
  (ii) Explain why air mass B would bring cold, wet weather.   **(2 KU marks)**

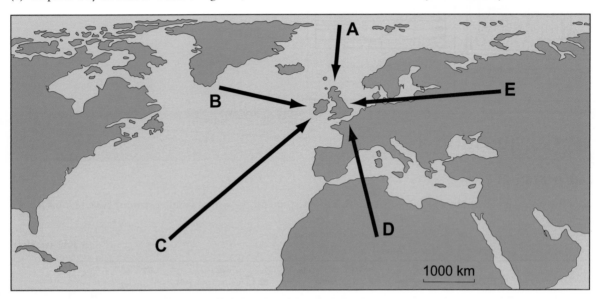

1000 km

General answer 2

*(i)   D is a tropical continental air mass, so it is likely to bring warm (✓)
       and dry (✓) weather to Britain.*

*(ii) B is an Arctic maritime air mass, so it will bring cold weather to Britain
       because it is coming from the north (✓), and it will also bring wet
       weather because it will pick up moisture as it passes over the ocean (✓).
       This could cause snow in winter (✓).*

Look out for

This sample answer illustrates the difference between a
'describe' and an 'explain' question. In part (i), you only
need to give a description of the weather conditions,
but in part (ii) you must give reasons to back up your
answers. The word 'explain' is often highlighted in bold
to alert you to this.

Look out for

Tropical air masses bring warm weather,
polar air masses bring cold weather, and
Arctic air masses are very cold! Maritime
air masses bring precipitation, whereas
continental air masses are usually drier.

General question 3

Features of a Stevenson Screen

Look at the diagram below. which shows some design features of a Stevenson Screen which is used to house thermometers.

Choose **three** of these features and for each **explain** why it is necessary. **(3 KU marks)**

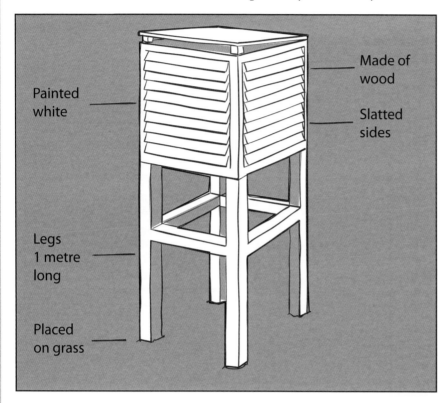

Painted white

Made of wood

Slatted sides

Legs 1 metre long

Placed on grass

General answer 3

First feature: painted white
Explanation: to reflect the sun's rays and give a more accurate temperature reading (✔).

Second feature: slatted sides
Explanation: to ensure that air can pass in and out of the box so that it doesn't heat up inside (✔).

Third feature: legs 1 metre long.
Explanation: to ensure that the thermometers inside the Stevenson screen measure the air temperature. If they were closer to the ground, they would measure the ground temperature (✔).

In this question, there are three parts and only three marks. You must answer all three parts to get full marks.

Forecasting the weather

What you should know at **General** **and** **Credit** **level …**

You will need to be able to recognise and know the meaning of weather symbols which are in common usage in many newspapers and on TV weather forecasts. You must also be able to read synoptic charts and symbols as used by the Meteorological Office and be able to predict weather conditions by interpreting these charts. To do this, you must understand the effects of different air masses, high- and low-pressure systems and weather fronts on the weather conditions at different places.

Diagram 8a: <u>Synoptic chart symbols (wind speed)</u>

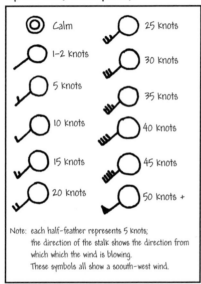

Note: each half-feather represents 5 knots;
the direction of the stalk shows the direction from which which the wind is blowing.
These symbols all show a soouth-west wind.

Diagram 8b:
<u>Synoptic chart symbols (cloud cover)</u>

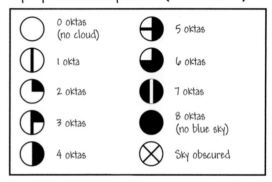

Diagram 8c:
<u>Synoptic chart symbols (precipitation)</u>

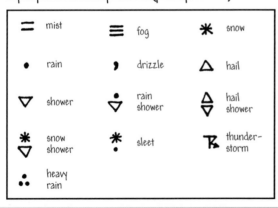

Diagram 8d: <u>Synoptic chart symbols</u>

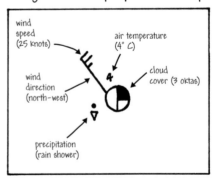

! Look out for

Wind is always named after the direction **from** which it blows. A north wind comes from the north (bringing cool air in Britain) and blows towards the south.

Diagram 9: <u>Weather fronts</u>

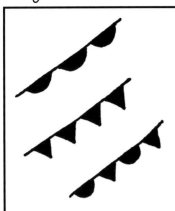

Weather conditions associated with the passage of a front

warm front: spell of prolonged rain, rise in temperature.

cold front: towering cumulonimbus clouds, short heavy rain showers, fall in temperature.

occluded front: blustery winds, heavy squally showers, sometimes of hail, thunder storms.

Diagram 10: <u>Pressure systems</u>

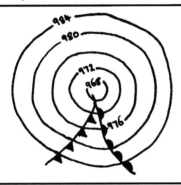
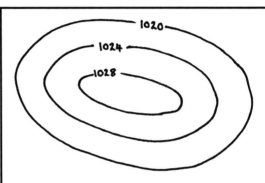

<u>Low pressure (depression)</u>	<u>High pressure (anticyclone)</u>
Isobar values decrease towards centre	Isobar values increase towards centre
Isobars are nearly circular	Isobars are elliptical (oval-shaped)
Isobars are tightly packed	Isobars are widely spaced
Winds travel anti-clockwise around the centre	Winds travel clockwise around the centre
Usually wet and windy weather (isobars close together)	Usually dry and less windy weather (isobars further apart)
Fronts bring rapid changes in the weather	Usually no fronts, so stable weather conditions

Look out for

Use the detailed glossary at the back of book to look up the meaning of words you are not sure about.

General question 4

Janice's Radio Phone-in

Look at the diagrams below.
Explain the different weather experiences which Janice's two callers had on 10 August 2004.   **(4 KU marks)**

General answer 4

Magnus has good weather in Shetland because there is high pressure
(✓), which is likely to bring clear sunny weather because it is August (✓)
and there are no fronts near, so it is dry (✓). Linda in Dunkeld has wet
weather because there is an occluded front close by (✓), which usually
brings the worst type of weather, including heavy rain (✓).

In synoptic chart questions, look out for the date, which will help to give you an idea of the
type of weather there is likely to be. If the date is January, the weather is not likely to be hot,
even in the warm sector! High pressure in January is likely to bring sunny, clear but cold and
frosty weather. In July, high pressure would bring hot sunny conditions.

Credit question 1

Synoptic Chart 12 noon, 18 November 2006

Look at the diagrams below.
Which set of weather information, X or Y, is correct for Bristol?
Explain your choice in detail. **(5 KU marks)**

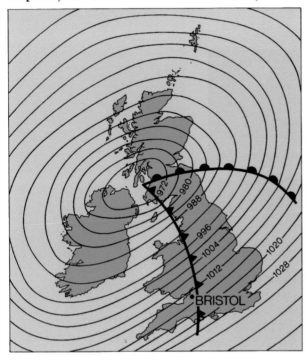

Two sets of weather information

	Set X	Set Y
Temperature	5°C	12°C
Wind speed	35 knots	10 knots
Wind direction	SW	E
Precipitation	Heavy rain	Steady rain
Cloud amount	7 oktas	4 oktas
Cloud type	Cumulonimbus	Stratus

Credit answer 1

Set X is the correct weather information (✓). This is because Bristol lies in the cold sector behind the cold front, which corresponds with the lower temperature of 5 degrees (✓). Bristol is still very close to the cold front, so you would expect there to be heavy rain (✓); and the isobars are very close, so the stronger wind speed of 35 knots fits well (✓). As wind travels anticlockwise around low-pressure zones, the SW wind direction is more accurate than the easterly direction shown in Set Y (✓). There are usually towering shower clouds at the cold front, so cumulonimbus is a better choice than stratus shown in Set Y (✓).

As this is a Knowledge question, there is a mark for identifying the correct set of data. To gain the other marks, you must be able to show knowledge of the weather conditions associated with low pressure and a cold front in particular (✓).

 **Look out for**

Remember that cloud cover is measured in **oktas** (eighths).

Credit question 2

European Synoptic Chart for noon, 8 July

Look at the diagram below.

On July 8th Mr McCormack is taking his young family to Blackpool for a one week holiday.

Do you think the weather conditions will be favourable for them?

Give reasons for your answer. **(5 ES marks)**

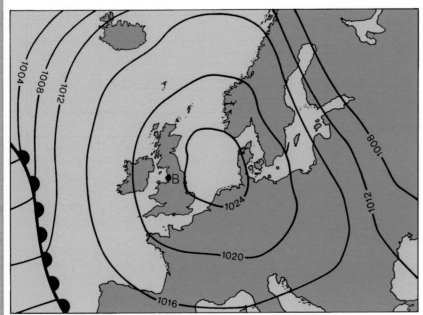

● B – Blackpool

Credit answer 2

The weather conditions could be very good because there is a large area of high pressure centred over Britain (✓), which is likely to bring clear, sunny weather (✓). The isobars are widely spaced, so there will not be much wind (✓), but what wind there is will be coming from the south, as wind travels clockwise around high pressure (✓). This will help to keep the temperatures up (✓). However, there is the threat of rain if the warm front moves in from the west (✓). This could also cause cloudy and cooler weather (✓).

Note that, in a 'choice' question such as this, you may be able to gain extra marks by giving both sides of the argument. This answer starts by saying that the weather will be favourable and giving the reasons why, but finishes by pointing out that there could be a change in the weather conditions and explaining why this might happen.

Look out for

Learn these facts about wind! Wind blows **anticlockwise** around the centre of a **low**-pressure system. It blows **clockwise** around the centre of a **high**-pressure system. Wind usually blows roughly parallel to the isobars.

KEY IDEA 3

The world can be divided into major climatic zones.

KEY IDEA 6

The physical environment is a resource which has to be used with care, and its management is a global issue.

Climate regions

What you should know at **General** level...

You need to know about the four main climate regions: **tundra**, **hot deserts**, **Mediterranean** and **tropical rain forests**. You will be expected to recognise and describe climate graphs of each of these regions. This involves the accurate interpretation of climate graphs by correctly identifying maximum and minimum temperatures and precipitation, as well as being able to calculate the **range of temperature**. The location of each region, as well as the opportunities and difficulties which these climates create for people, can also form the basis for questions on Key Idea 3.

General question 1

Tropical Rainforest Climate

Look at the diagram.
Describe, in detail, the climate of the tropical rainforest.

(3 ES marks)

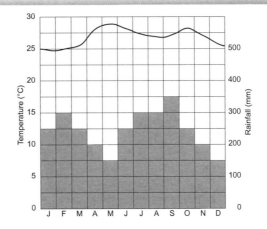

General answer 1

The temperature is hot all year round (✓), varying from a minimum 25 degrees Centigrade in January and February (✓) to a maximum 29 degrees Centigrade in May (✓). This gives a temperature range of just 4 degrees Centigrade (✓). It is very wet all year round (✓), with a maximum precipitation of 350 millimetres in September (✓).

Look out for

A good answer to a climate graph question will identify overall patterns as well as maximum and minimum temperatures and rainfall levels. It is important to include references both to temperature and to precipitation to ensure full marks. If you calculate the range of temperature, this will always gain a mark.

Look out for

The range of temperature = highest monthly temperature minus the lowest monthly temperature.

General question 2

Climate Graphs for Selected Regions

Look at the diagrams below.
Both regions X and Y are sparsely populated.
Referring to the climate information, **explain** why it is difficult for people to live and work in each of these regions.

(4 ES marks)

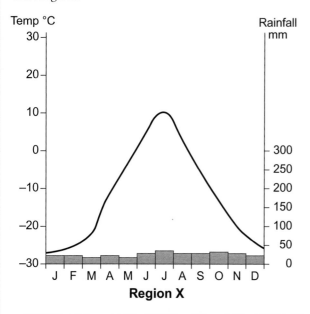

Region X

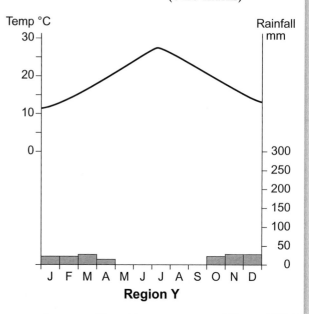

Region Y

General answer 2

Region X is difficult for people to live in because it is tundra (✓). The cold temperatures mean that everything is frozen for most of the year (✓) and it is not possible to grow crops (✓). Roads may be blocked with snow (✓), and it is difficult to get water because of the sub-zero temperatures (✓).

Region Y is difficult for people to live in because it is hot desert (✓). The main problem is drought (✓), making it difficult to farm or keep animals (✓). The high temperatures make it very uncomfortable to do many jobs (✓).

In this answer, marks can be gained by correctly identifying the climate regions because their names have not been given in the question. Hot deserts and tundra regions are well known as hostile environments for people. To gain further marks, you just need to give some examples of the ways in which the climate creates difficulties.

You must also be able to identify the approximate locations of each of the four main climate types on an outline world map.

Environmental problems

What you should know at General **and** Credit **level …**

As well as knowledge of climate graphs for each of the four regions, you must know about environmental problems affecting tropical rainforests, hot deserts and the world's oceans. In particular, you might have to answer questions about **deforestation**, **desertification**, **marine pollution** and the problems caused by the **exploitation** of these environments (e.g. overfishing). Related environmental problems such as **global warming** are linked to these issues. You will be expected to be able to suggest ways in which the factors causing these problems can be reduced.

General question 3

Developments in the Rainforests of Brazil

Look at the diagrams below.
'Developments in rainforests have brought many benefits to local people.'
Do you agree with the above statement?
Explain your answer. **(4 ES marks)**

General answer 3

There have been both benefits and problems caused by developments in the rainforest (✓). Local people will have gained jobs (✓), and also there will be better transport with the new roads (✓). However, there will also have been many problems, as these developments have caused many trees to be cut down (✓), causing the loss of animal habitats (✓). The building of dams will flood a lot of land (✓), and the loss of trees will lead to global warming (✓), as there is less forest to absorb carbon dioxide (✓).

This answer shows how it is possible to gain marks by partly agreeing and partly disagreeing with the statement.

Credit question 1

Brazilian Rainforest Facts

'Cutting down the rainforest in Brazil will affect the whole world more than it will affect Brazil itself.' – Statement by an environmental spokesperson

Look at the diagram below.

To what extent do you agree with the statement?

Give reasons for your answer.   **(6 ES marks)**.

Mineral resources	Largest number of plant and animal species of any natural region
Native American Indians living on reserves	Hydro-electric power potential
Valuable hardwood timber	Cattle ranching and plantation agriculture
In-migration of settlers	Trees convert carbon dioxide to oxygen
Medicines derived from plants	Trans-Amazonian highway opening up remote areas

Credit answer 1

There will be effects both on local people and on the whole world. Local tribes will be affected because they will lose their land (✓), and their whole way of life will be at risk if too much forest is destroyed (✓). Living on a reserve will restrict their freedom when previously they had the whole rainforest(✓). If settlers migrate into areas which have been felled and try to graze cattle on the land, they may destroy the land further (✓) as the heavy tropical rains wash away the minerals, causing the soil to become infertile (✓) and eventually washing away the topsoil altogether (✓). Some of the effects of these developments will be global. For example, deforestation can lead to increased global warming (✓), as there will be fewer trees to absorb carbon dioxide (✓), and burning trees will also give off more carbon dioxide (✓). The loss of trees will prevent the discovery of new medicines derived from plants, and this will have a global impact (✓).

Note that, in this answer, there is no credit for agreeing or disagreeing with the statement. Marks are awarded for giving reasons as to why it may or may not be true. It is quite OK to partially agree and partially disagree which this answer does.

Look out for

Deforestation in places such the Amazon and South-East Asia is a major contributor to global warming through the loss of trees, which absorb carbon dioxide, and because so many areas of forest are burned down, leading to the release of yet more carbon dioxide.

Credit question 2

Desertification

Look at the diagram below.

(a) Desertification is a major problem in many areas of the world.
Choose **one** physical and **one** human cause and **explain** why each of them is a major reason for desertification. **(4 KU marks)**

(b) **Describe**, in detail, ways in which desertification can be overcome **(4 KU marks)**

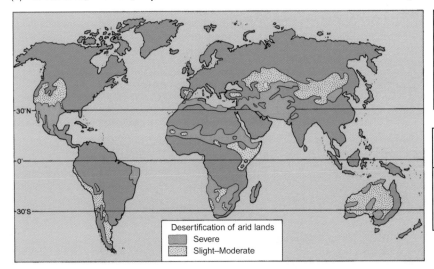

Physical Causes of Desertification
Unreliable rainfall
Wind
High temperatures

Human Causes of Desertification
Population increase
Overgrazing/overcropping
Removing trees for firewood

Desertification of arid lands
■ Severe
▨ Slight–Moderate

Credit answer 2

a) Unreliable rainfall is a major physical cause of desertification. Without sufficient rainfall, plants wither and die, causing the soil to be exposed (✓). As the soil is very dry, it can be easily picked up by the wind and blown away (✓). The land can become irreparably damaged and turn to desert (✓).

Population increase is a major human reason for desertification in some places. As the population in an area grows, marginal land which cannot really support agriculture will be cultivated (✓). This land may be too fragile and is easily destroyed by human activity (✓). If farmers increase the number of cattle in the area, they may cause overgrazing, resulting in the destruction of the natural vegetation cover (✓). This will lead to the soil being exposed to wind or heavy rain, causing soil erosion and eventually desertification (✓).

b) Desertification can be overcome in a number of ways. If there is sufficient water, irrigation can be used (✓). This will help to keep the soil moist so that it can't dry out and blow away (✓); also, it will keep the vegetation healthy, which will keep a protective cover over the soil (✓).

Planting shrubs, trees or bushes on vulnerable areas will help to protect the soil as the roots grow longer and help to bind the soil together (✓). When the trees grow, they will shade the soil and keep it more moist (✓). Finding alternative fuel sources for cooking can help to prevent desertification, as there will be less deforestation (✓).

> In a Knowledge question such as this, you must know at least two different ways of limiting desertification and be able to describe them in some detail.

Credit question 3

Threats to the Marine Environment around Scotland

What measures could be taken to reduce the impact of the threats to the marine environment as shown on the diagram below?   **(6 KU marks)**

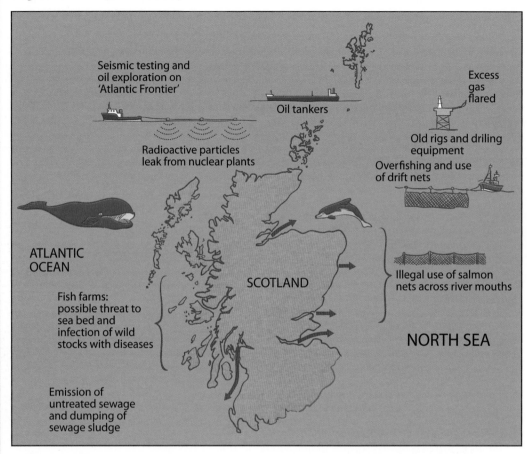

Seismic testing and oil exploration on 'Atlantic Frontier'

Oil tankers

Excess gas flared

Radioactive particles leak from nuclear plants

Old rigs and driling equipment

Overfishing and use of drift nets

ATLANTIC OCEAN

SCOTLAND

Illegal use of salmon nets across river mouths

Fish farms: possible threat to sea bed and infection of wild stocks with diseases

NORTH SEA

Emission of untreated sewage and dumping of sewage sludge

It is not necessary to find something to say about every problem shown on the diagram, so long as you make plenty of valid points about some of them.

Credit answer 3

There are many things which could be done to reduce the impact of the threats to the marine environment. New laws have been introduced to ensure that new oil tankers are now double-hulled to reduce the threat of oil spills (✓). Fish quotas have been introduced by the EU to reduce overfishing (✓), and boats now use new types of net to allow younger fish to escape (✓). Fishing boats have to tie up for a certain number of days each month to reduce overfishing (✓). EU laws have made it illegal to discharge untreated sewage from towns into the sea (✓), so now much more is properly cleaned up in sewage-treatment works (✓). There have been proposals to establish marine reserves around the UK to protect endangered species such as whales (✓). Excess gas from oil rigs can be used for heating instead of being burned off into the atmosphere (✓).

These two Key Ideas are similar, the main difference being that, in Key Idea 4, questions may be about any part of the world, whereas, in Key Idea 5, questions will be mainly about land-use conflicts in Scotland.

The physical environment offers a range of possibilities for, and limitations on, human activity.

There are many competing demands for the use of rural landscapes.

Land use conflicts

What you should know at **General** **and** **Credit** **level …**

Questions will be about the relationship between the physical environment and people. You should understand what a **land use conflict** is (i.e. how the interests of different land users may not be able to exist easily together in the same location). You should have some knowledge of the **National Parks** (especially in Scotland), their aims, possible land use conflicts and ways in which these can be resolved. You should also understand the concept of **conservation** and how this might affect other land users. These Key Ideas are often covered within the map questions.

General question 1

Landscapes of the Tay Valley

Explain why land use along the River Tay is different in the two diagrams. **(4 KU marks)**

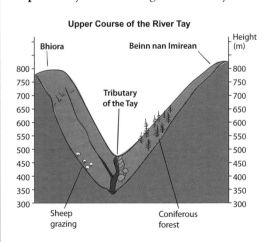

Upper Course of the River Tay

Bhiora Beinn nan Imirean

Height (m)

Tributary of the Tay

800, 750, 700, 650, 600, 550, 500, 450, 400, 350, 300

Sheep grazing Coniferous forest

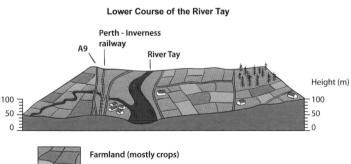

Lower Course of the River Tay

Perth - Inverness railway

A9 River Tay

Height (m)

100, 50, 0

Farmland (mostly crops)

Coniferous woodland

General answer 1

Land in the upper course is too steep for arable farming but can still be used for trees (✓), whereas the land along the lower course is flatter and is suitable for farm machinery and arable farming (✓). Also, the land in the lower course is partly flood plain and so would have deep and fertile soil, which is good for farming (✓), whereas the soils on the steep slopes of the upper course will be thin and unsuitable for farming (✓). There is more settlement in the lower course because the land is flat and easier to build on (✓) and also has good transport links (✓), whereas the land in the upper course has neither of these advantages (✓).

This is an 'explain' question, so to get marks you must give reasons. Also, because the question asks why land use is different in the upper and lower sections, your answers must refer to both sections of the river. It is easy to misinterpret this question and just describe the differences, which would not achieve any marks.

Credit question 1

Land Use Conflict in Loch Lomond and Trossachs National Park

Study the diagram below.
Select two different land uses.
Explain in detail why they may be in conflict with each other.   **(5 KU marks)**

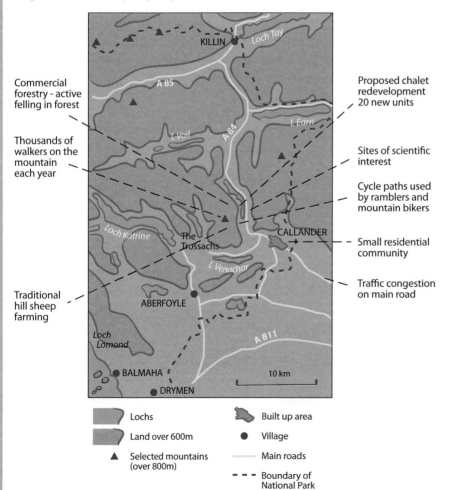

Credit answer 1

The two different land uses are traditional hill sheep-farming and hillwalking,

Hill sheep-farmers may not be keen on thousands of hillwalkers, because they could drop litter which may harm the sheep (✓). Walkers could also leave gates open, allowing sheep to escape (✓), and they may also damage fences and walls by trying to climb over them, putting the farmer to the extra expense of repairing them (✓). At lambing time, ewes may get stressed if walkers come too close (✓), particularly if they allow their dogs to run without a lead (✓).

From the walkers' point of view, hill sheep-farming may be a problem if there are areas which they cannot access for walking in (✓); and walls and barbed-wire fences create obstacles for walkers which are difficult to cross if there are no stiles (✓). Walkers could have their dogs shot by a farmer if they allow them to worry the sheep (✓).

This is a good answer because it sticks to just two different land uses, as the question stipulates. It is important to say which two you have chosen right at the start. If more than two land uses were referred to, you would still only get marks for the best two. It makes more valid points than there are marks available, so it easily scores full marks. When identifying possible conflicts, the answer is clearly explained. For example, instead of just saying that gates might be left open, the answer explains why this is a problem – the sheep might escape! It is essential to make sure that you give detailed reasons in all 'explain' questions such as this.

Credit question 2

Land Use Conflict in Loch Lomond and Trossachs National Park

A group of pupils wants to investigate land use conflicts in the National Park. Describe **two** gathering techniques they could use to collect appropriate data. Give reasons for your choice.

(6 ES marks)

This is a 'gathering techniques' question designed to test your knowledge of fieldwork methods. These can occur in any of the physical or human Key Ideas. You must be able to choose relevant fieldwork techniques and give reasons to explain why they are suitable.

Look out for

Loch Lomond and the Trossachs, along with the Cairngorms, are Scotland's two National Parks. Their aims include conserving the beauty of the landscape and protecting wildlife, but also encouraging access for visitors. This inevitably results in a variety of land use conflicts.

Credit answer 2

One gathering technique which they could use would be to interview different groups of people such as walkers and farmers (✓). This would allow the pupils to find out what each group's concerns are (✓), as they would be getting the information direct (first-hand) from the opposing groups of land users (✓).

The students could also take photos of areas where there might be environmental problems (✓). This would allow them, for example, to demonstrate the effects of footpath erosion caused by walkers or cyclists (✓). If the pupils could return to the site over several weeks or months, they could compare early photos with later ones to see how quickly erosion had taken place (✓). Photos could be labelled to highlight specific areas of concern (✓).

Look out for

'**Gathering** techniques' questions are about methods of **collecting** information to help carry out an investigation. '**Processing** techniques' questions are about different ways of **displaying** information once it has been collected.

As the question indicates that two gathering techniques must be described and their suitability explained, it is important to choose two but not any more than that. Marks will not be given for further examples of techniques. To score full marks, detailed explanations are needed. Note that, if you choose questionnaire or interview as one of your techniques, it is vital that you state to whom you would give the questions or whom you would interview. Without this information, you will not get the marks for your choice of technique. Good explanations of gathering techniques state how each one is useful and exactly how it will help to give results in a field study.

KEY IDEA 7

Settlements have many common characteristics related to site, situation and function.

KEY IDEA 8

Urban settlements have dynamic patterns relating to their size, form and function.

Urban geography

What you should know at **General** and **Credit** level ...

Urban geography is a topic which features in all the Standard Grade papers and is frequently tested via your knowledge of settlements on Ordnance Survey maps. From the evidence given on a map or diagram, you should be able to describe factors which have influenced the **site** of a settlement, such as the availability of water or being situated at a bridging point. You should know about the **functions** of settlements and be able to suggest from map evidence what these might be (e.g. port, market town, tourist centre). You must learn about the main land-use zones which occur in cities. These are the **Central Business District (CBD)**, the **inner city** and the **suburbs**. You will also be expected to know about the land around the edge of the city, called the **rural–urban fringe**, some of which may also be classed as **greenbelt** land. You should be able to describe the urban landscape of each zone and to give reasons for the differences. The higher price of land closer to the city centre is a key reason for the different land use in each zone. You must be able to recognise each of the zones on map extracts and to give evidence which backs up your choice of zone (see Chapter 10 on map skills).

Diagram 11: Urban zones

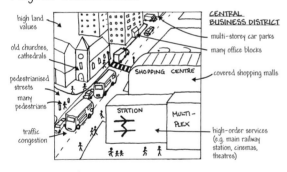

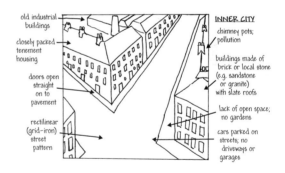

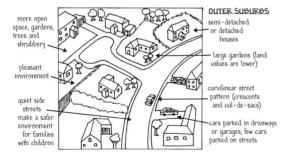

The **sphere of influence** of a settlement is the area around it from which people travel to use its services. A small settlement will have only **low-order services** such as a village shop, and so its sphere of influence will be small (perhaps just a few miles). A market town might have **medium-order services** such as supermarkets, which people will travel a fair distance to use. A city will have **high-order services** such as an international airport and theatres, which people will travel long distances to make use of. Therefore, cities have very large spheres of influence, which can easily stretch for 100 miles or more beyond the city boundary. The size and shape of the sphere of influence for any given settlement will depend on its population, its services and how close it is to other settlements.

General question 1

Land Uses at the Edge of a City

Look at the diagram below.

Choose **one** of the main land uses in the diagram – A, B or C.

Explain why the edge of the city is a good location for this land use. **(3 KU marks)**

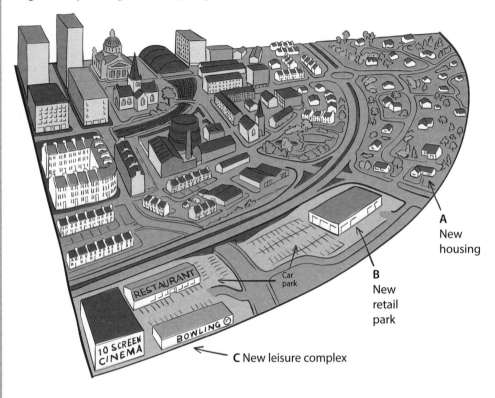

A New housing

B New retail park

C New leisure complex

Car park

RESTAURANT

10 SCREEN CINEMA

BOWLING ☺

General answer 1

A (new housing) is often found at the edge of the city because the land is cheaper there (✓) and there will be more space for the houses to have gardens (✓). Also, it is more likely to be a pleasant environment away from the middle of the city (✓), but it will still be close enough for people to commute to work in the centre (✓).

Good answers about urban land use will make reference to land values.

General question 2

Land Uses at the Edge of a City

Identify two techniques which pupils could use to gather information in a study of an out–of–town shopping centre. Give reasons for your choice. **(4 ES marks)**

General answer 2

Technique 1: interview shop managers (✓)
Technique 2: survey of shop types (✓)

The pupils could interview a number of shop managers to find out why they decided to locate in the shopping centre (✓). This would tell them the advantages of the centre for businesses (✓). Pupils could visit and record the types of shop which are present to see how many different types of shop there are (✓). This would let them see what the most common types are (e.g. shoe shops) (✓).

In 'gathering techniques' questions, it is important to give reasons for the techniques you choose. Say which people will be interviewed and why it would be useful. You must be clear about what is being surveyed and say how this information would help the study.

General question 3

Two Housing Areas in Liverpool

Look at the areas A and B below.

Describe the differences in housing density and street patterns between the two areas **(3 ES marks)**.

A

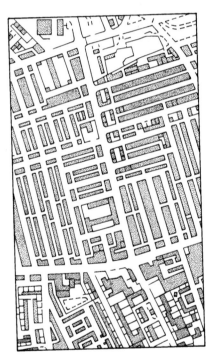

B

General answer 3

Area A has densely packed housing which is built in a grid-iron street pattern, whereas Area B is more spread out (✓) and is built in a curvilinear pattern (✓).

Area A has little space for gardens around the houses, in contrast to Area B (✓). Area B also has room for cars to be parked in the driveways, whereas in Area A the cars would be parked in the street because there is no other room (✓).

This is a 'describe' question, and there is no need for explanations. Notice that marks are only awarded here where clear differences are described. It is good practice in this type of question to compare each area so that the differences are clearly stated.

Look out for

Remember that **inner-city** areas have grid-iron (**rectilinear**) street patterns, while **suburban** streets are often set out with crescents and cul-de-sacs (**curvilinear**).

Credit question 1

Land Use in a Scottish City

Look at the diagrams below.
Give reasons for the patterns of the land use shown in both the suburbs and the Central Business District. **(6 KU marks)**

Suburbs

Central Business District

▨	Residential
⦀	Hotels
▦	Public Buildings
▨	Shops
☐	Open space
⊙	Offices
⦂	Entertainment
⊠	Industry

Credit answer 1

The CBD has lots of shops, but the suburbs don't because shop owners want to locate in the most accessible part of the city, which is usually the CBD (✓). This will allow them to attract more customers than they would anywhere else in the city (✓) and therefore make more profit (✓). There is no open space in the CBD, whereas about 20% of land in the suburbs is open space, because land in the centre is much more valuable (✓) and land owners will use every scrap of land to build on to get a return for the high prices they will have paid for it (✓). Three quarters of the land in the suburbs is used for housing, but there's none in the centre because land values are much lower in the suburbs, and people can afford to build there (✓) and have space around their house for a garden and a garage (✓).

Unlike the last question (sample General answer 3), this is an 'explain' question, and so, as well as pointing out what the differences are between the CBD and the suburbs, the response has to give reasons for these differences. It is essential in an 'explain' question that you use phrases such as 'because' and 'due to'.

Credit question 2

Central Business District of a Large City

Study the diagram below.
In recent years many changes have taken place in the Central Business Districts of British cities. Give reasons for these changes. **(5 KU marks)**

Credit answer 2

Roads in the CBD have been pedestrianised to make them safer for shoppers (✓). It will also be more pleasant without the noise and fumes from traffic (✓). Many roads have been made one-way, along with other changes to try to reduce traffic congestion (✓). Often, these changes include improving public transport, by making bus services better for example, in order to persuade people to leave their cars at home, so reducing the amount of traffic (✓). Many older buildings have been redeveloped or demolished and replaced by new office blocks as developers try to make a profit by selling space to companies in a desirable location (✓). Multi-storey car parks have been built to reduce on-street parking and help to improve traffic flow (✓).

It is important to make sure that you give explanations here and don't fall into the trap of just describing the changes, as this is an 'explain' question. Also, you can give explanations for other changes which you know of. You don't have to stick to the changes shown in the diagram; use your knowledge too!

 **Look out for**

Many urban questions refer to Ordnance Survey map extracts. Check out the section on urban map questions in Chapter 10.

KEY IDEA 9

Farming systems provide food supplies and raw materials.

Farming

What you should know at **General** and **Credit** level ...

You need to know about the main farming types: **arable**, **pastoral** and **mixed**. Farmers decide how they will use their land, depending on physical factors such as relief, climate and soil, and on human factors such as distance to market, labour force and government grants. Farms can be considered as systems; think of them as open-air factories with inputs such as technology, seeds and fertiliser and with outputs such as crops, animals and wool. There are some farming words that you should know to help you give explanations in your answers. Words and phrases such as **fodder** and **crop rotation** are terms you should learn the meaning of. You should be able to identify the advantages and disadvantages of a farm's location by studying evidence on an Ordnance Survey map.

Over the last few decades, farms have experienced a lot of changes, and you must be able to give examples of these and explain the reasons for them.

The increased use of machinery, reduction in the workforce and the use of chemical fertilisers are examples of these changes. **Farm diversification** is when farms branch out into activities which are different from traditional food production. Examples of this would be running bed-and-breakfast, renting out holiday cottages or offering pony trekking.

General question 1

Brockan Farm

Study the diagrams below and on page 35.
Suggest reasons for the changes shown on Brockan Farm between 1977 and 2007.   **(4 KU marks)**

Brockan Farm in 1977

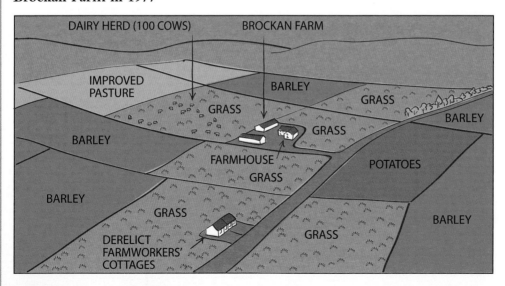

Brockan Farm in 2007

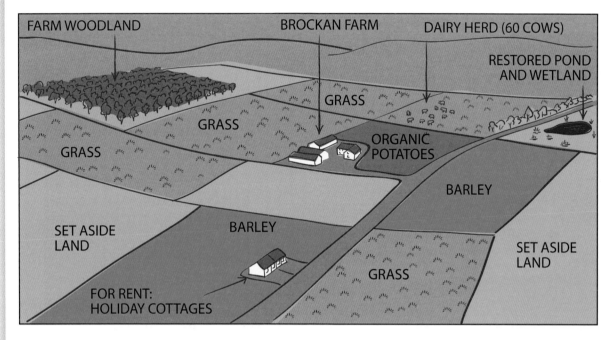

General answer 1

Some of the field boundaries have been removed to make the fields bigger so that machinery can work more easily (✓). This is also more efficient for the farmer, as it gives some extra land to be farmed (✓). The farmer has planted woodland in some fields because there may have been government or EU grants to do this (✓). Old farmworkers' cottages have been converted into holiday cottages to rent out. This is because most of the work is now done by machine, and the farmworkers are no longer needed (✓). The cottages bring in extra income for the farmer (✓).

 **Look out for**

Farmers can play a big role in helping to protect the environment. This can often be the reason for some of the changes in farming as farms receive grants for a variety of environmentally friendly activities such as set-aside and farm woodland schemes.

To pick up marks, it is essential to give reasons for the changes. A detailed explanation can pick up two marks, as shown in the last two sentences about the reasons for the change in use of the cottages.

General question 2

Recent Trends in Farming

'Recent trends in farming are of great benefit to the British people.'
Do you agree? Explain your answer.   **(4 ES marks)**

Organic crops

Chemical fertilisers

GM crops

Diversification

Larger fields

This is an Enquiry Skills question, where you are asked to give a view on the statement and to justify it. It is OK to say that you partly agree, so long as you give reasons both for and against the statement. Sometimes this might make it easier to gain marks.

General answer 2

I partly agree with the statement. Farms producing organic crops are good for the environment, as fewer chemicals are used (✓) and they are healthier for people to eat (✓). Diversification might also be good for the British people, as the farm may be offering services for tourists such as bed-and-breakfast (✓) or doing things to help the environment such as planting trees (✓). On the other hand, I disagree with the statement because larger fields may mean that animal habitats in hedgerows have been destroyed (✓); and many people are against the introduction of GM crops (✓).

Credit question 1

Inverlochlarig Sheep Farm, Perthshire

'I'm so fed up with ever increasing fuel costs, lower prices from animal sales and dealing with the EU that I wonder if it is worth carrying on.' – Local farmer

Study the diagram below.

Human and physical factors both create problems for farmers in this type of environment. Select **either** human **or** physical factors. For the factors you have chosen **explain**, in detail, why these cause more problems for the farmer.

(6 ES marks)

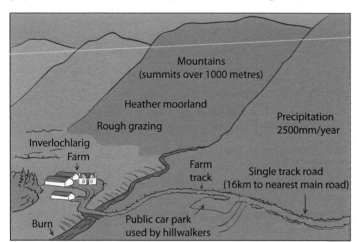

Credit answer 1

Human factors are likely to cause more problems for the farmer at Inverlochlarig. For example, walkers are likely to cause difficulty for the farm, as they may damage fences and walls as they climb over them (✓), and they may drop litter which could potentially harm livestock(✓). Increasing tourist traffic on the single-track road may cause problems for farm vehicles (✓), while variable prices at market will mean that income from animal sales is unreliable (✓). To obtain EU grants, there is an ever-increasing amount of paperwork to complete, which will take up time (✓); and the rules on what grants are given for keep changing, so this makes it difficult for the farmer to plan (✓). Rising fuel prices are likely to reduce the farm's profits (✓). Physical factors are less likely to change, and so the farmer will experience more difficulty because of the rapid changes in human factors (✓).

*In this answer, you must choose one set of factors and stick to them, as the question asks you to choose **either** human **or** physical factors. In this case, you should **not** try to give both sides of the argument, as you will only be given marks for one set of factors. As always, in Enquiry Skills questions, there are no marks for your choice. You have to give valid supporting reasons to gain marks.*

Try to make **developed** statements whenever you can in your answers.

This is where one part of your answer to a question is so well explained that it merits two marks. An example of a developed explanation, worth two marks, would be:

'Frequent snow causes difficulty at Inverlochlarig farm in winter because it can block the road to the farm (✓), making it impossible for goods to be taken to market or supplies to be delivered (✓).'

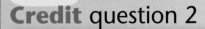

Credit question 2

Physical Data for two Farms in Scotland

Look at the tables below.
Give reasons for the differences between the two farms.   **(6 ES marks)**

	Farm A	Farm B
Altitude	220 m to 450 m	75 m to 125 m
Average rainfall per year	1520 mm	630 mm
Sunshine hours per year	1000	1300

	Farm A	Farm B
Area	1904 ha	444 ha
Workers	3 full time	5 full time 13 part time/seasonal
Machinery	2 tractors 8 other machines	6 tractors 14 other machines
Land use	80% sheep grazing 13% beef cattle grazing 7% barley, turnips and hay	87% arable – mainly wheat and barley with some potatoes, raspberries 13% beef cattle grazing

Credit answer 2

The data shows that Farm A mainly keeps animals, whereas Farm B mainly grows crops. This will probably be because Farm A has a lot of high land (up to 450 metres), so it is likely to have a lot of steep land, making it harder to grow crops than at Farm B, where the land appears to be low (✓). The high land at Farm A will also make for lower temperatures than at Farm B, which will therefore have more favourable temperatures (✓). The high rainfall levels at Farm A would also make the ground wet and difficult to work, whereas Farm B has less rainfall but still enough for crops to grow (✓). Farm B has more hours of sunshine than Farm A, so the crops would ripen better here (✓). Farm B has 87% of its land given over to arable farming, whereas Farm B has only 7%. This will be because Farm B earns most of its income from producing crops, whereas Farm A is likely only to use its crops for fodder (✓). Farm B has more workers than at A because there is more machinery to operate (✓), and at Farm A the sheep will not need much attention for long periods of time (✓).

This is a difficult question, and you need to break it down into sections. Say what the differences are, and remember that you will not gain any marks until you give reasons for the differences. It is easiest to take one difference at a time and clearly state how each factor affects the two farms. Note that this answer quotes figures from the tables to highlight the differences.

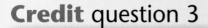

Credit question 3

Physical Data for two Farms in Scotland

Look at the tables below.
Describe other techniques which could be used to present the land use data shown.
Give reasons for your choice of techniques. **(5 ES marks)**

	Farm A	Farm B
Altitude	220 m to 450 m	75 m to 125 m
Average rainfall per year	1520 mm	630 mm
Sunshine hours per year	1000	1300

	Farm A	Farm B
Area	1904 ha	444 ha
Workers	3 full time	5 full time
13 part time/seasonal
Machinery	2 tractors
8 other machines	6 tractors
14 other machines
Land use	80% sheep grazing
13% beef cattle grazing
7% barley, turnips and hay	87% arable – mainly wheat
and barley with some potatoes,
raspberries
13% beef cattle grazing

In this 'processing techniques' question, it is important to note that it is only the land use data (at the bottom of the second table) that you are being asked to compare. You are asked to give other techniques, so you will need to give at least two; but it might be easier to pick up marks if you can think of three. Full marks will only be given if your techniques are valid and you give reasons to explain why they are suitable. Try not to use the same reasons twice.

Credit answer 3

The land use data could be shown on two pie charts (✓) because the figures are already in percentages (✓). The two graphs could be displayed side by side and different colours used for each land use to make comparison easy (✓).

A bar chart could also be used for this information (✓) with a different-coloured bar for each farm, so that, where they have the same land use, the differences between the two farms could be quickly identified (✓). A pictogram would be another possible way of showing the data (✓), as the images would display the land uses being compared, thereby reducing the need for words (✓).

Look out for

Farming questions can also appear on Ordnance Survey map extracts. See page 90 for an example.

KEY IDEA 10

The viability of manufacturing industry is affected by a variety of factors.

KEY IDEA 11

Economic change has social and environmental consequences.

Industry

What you should know at **General** and **Credit** level ...

There are three main types of industry that you need to know about.

Primary industry involves producing food or extracting things from the land or sea. This type of industry produces raw materials. Farming, fishing and mining are examples of primary industry.

Secondary industry takes raw materials and produces goods from them. It is often known as manufacturing industry. Steelmaking and car production are examples of secondary industry.

Tertiary industry provides services for people to use. Nurses, teachers and newsagents are examples of people working in tertiary (service) industries.

You must know about the main influences on the location of industries. These are called industrial location factors and are shown in this diagram. Often, the importance of each factor changes over time.

Diagram 12: <u>Industrial location factors</u>

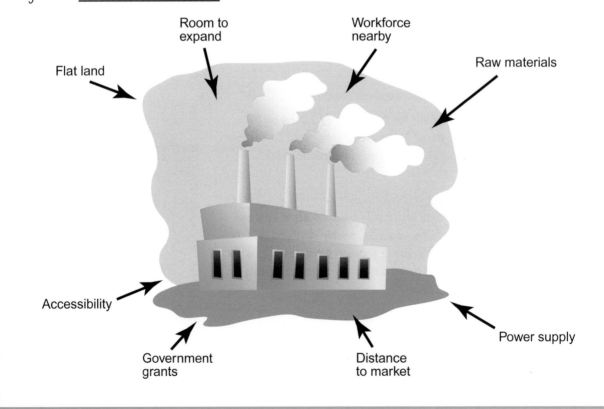

General question 1

A Modern Industrial Landscape

Look at the diagram below.

Explain why some of the labelled features are typical of a modern industrial landscape. **(4 KU marks)**

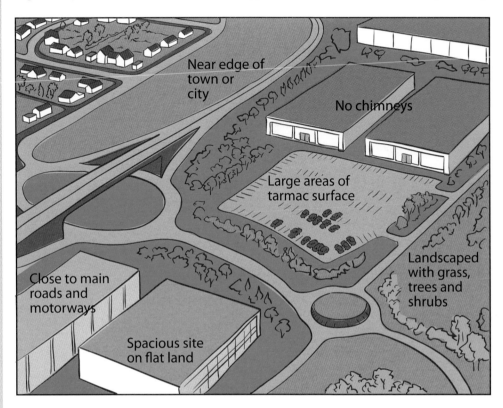

Near edge of town or city

No chimneys

Large areas of tarmac surface

Landscaped with grass, trees and shrubs

Close to main roads and motorways

Spacious site on flat land

General answer 1

A modern industrial landscape doesn't usually have any chimneys, because the factories use electricity now (✓). They need to be close to main roads or motorways because they depend on good road transport to deliver their products (✓). They are often on the edges of cities because the land there is cheaper (✓), there is more space to build new factories (✓) and they are still close to a workforce (✓). Modern industrial landscapes are often landscaped to make a more attractive environment for people to work in (✓).

Notice that these statements are all explanations. It is easy to fall into the trap of just describing what is in the diagram; but you will gain very few marks if you do that. There is no need to explain every single feature in the diagram, so long as your answer explains some of them well.

Look out for

You may also have to answer an industry question using an Ordnance Survey map extract. See page 87 for an example of this.

General question 2

Location of a Cement Works

Study the diagram below.
Do you think this is a good location for a cement works?
Give reasons for your answer. **(4 ES marks)**

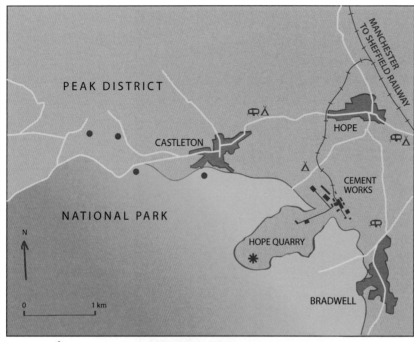

KEY

● Lime caves (open to the public)

🚐 Caravan site

Λ Campsite

▬ Built up area

┼─┼─ Railway

── Road

▨ Limestone hills

✳ LIMESTONE, THE MAIN RAW MATERIAL IN THE MANUFACTURE OF CEMENT

General answer 2

This is a good location for the cement works because it is close to limestone hills from where the main raw material can be obtained (✓). This will keep transport costs down (✓). There is also a railway into the site, so that the products can be transported out easily by train (✓), which will help to keep heavy goods vehicles off the roads (✓). The site is close to three villages, which could provide workers for the factory (✓). On the other hand, this site is in the Peak District National Park, where visitors will see it as an ugly blot on the landscape (✓).

*To answer this question successfully, you need to know the main industrial location factors. It is possible to answer 'yes' **or** 'no' to the question, so long as you clearly explain the reasons you give for doing so.*

Look out for

It is possible to partly agree and partly disagree with this type of question, providing you back up your statements with explanations.

Look out for

Make your explanations as clear as possible. Good industrial sites are on flat land because it is easier and cheaper to build on. Factories near main roads have an advantage because there is good access which allows delivery vehicles to deliver freight easily and quickly.

Credit question 1

Look at the diagrams below.

In your opinion, which **three** factors were most important in the location of the University of Southampton Science Park?

Give reasons to support your choice.   **(5 ES marks)**

Factors influencing the location of a Science Park

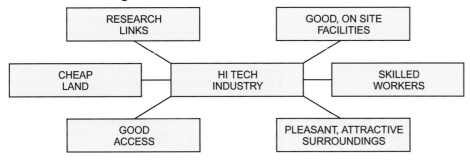

Location of University of Southampton Science Park

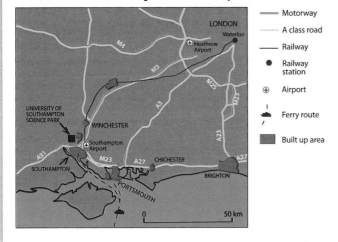

Site of University of Southampton Science Park

Credit answer 1

Being close to a university will be important for a science park because it will need highly trained workers, which the university can provide (✓). Companies on the science park may also be involved in research, which they could do in cooperation with the university (✓). Southampton University Science Park is surrounded by woodland, which makes it an attractive place to work; and this will be important to help attract the best workers (✓). This could help the companies on the science park compete with other locations to get the top experts to work for them (✓). Being situated close to the M3 and M23 motorways gives good road access, which is vital for firms in a science park, as they might need to have quick deliveries from all over the country (✓). Workers will also be able to get there easily (✓). It is also close to an international airport, which will help them to export goods and import them quickly from abroad (✓).

In this question, it is important to stick to three factors and to explain in detail why they are important. Choose factors that you can find plenty to say about. There will be no marks for the factors you choose, only for the explanations. Your answer must refer to Southampton University Science Park as the question asks.

Credit question 2

Look at the diagrams below.
What are the advantages of locating a car factory at Burnaston?   **(6 ES marks)**

Location of Toyota Car Factory at Burnaston

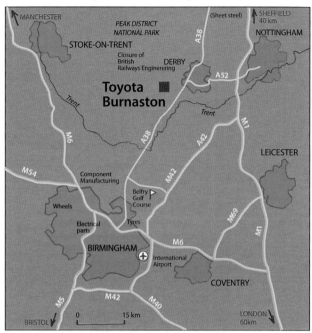

Site of Toyota Car Factory at Burnaston

Credit answer 2

Burnaston is a good location for a car factory because it is a large flat site which would have been easy to build on (✓), and also there is room round about to expand into (✓). As the land is outside the city, it will have been cheaper to buy (✓). There are firms in cities nearby, such as Birmingham and Sheffield, which manufacture parts such as tyres that would be needed in the car factory (✓).

Burnaston is close to Derby, where there would be a workforce (✓) and which, along with other cities which are not too far away, would provide a market for selling the cars (✓). There is good road access via the A38, and the MI motorway is not too far away, so importing parts and exporting cars will be easy (✓).

Notice that it is important to explain fully what the advantages are. For example, it is not enough to say that the access is good. You should also say how it is good (in this case, next to main roads, the A38 and MI) and why that is important. Similarly, it is not enough to say that there is flat land, unless you also add that this is good for building on.

Good access to rail transport is an advantage for many different industries. However, being next to a railway line will not help unless there are railway sidings for freight or a railway station. Study the resources you are given carefully to see whether or not this is the case before mentioning a railway.

Economic change

What you should know at General **and** Credit **level ...**

When large industries close down, unemployment will increase; but there are often more widespread effects for the local economy, community and environment. As fewer people have wage packets coming in, families have less money to spend, so local businesses are badly affected, and some may shut down. In order to find work, many families may have to move away. This can lead to a fall in house prices, and the area can be seen as depressed. Industrial sites can become derelict, and there may be environmental problems too. This series of events is known as a spiral of economic decline (see diagram). In order to prevent these problems from becoming too severe, government and EU grants are often given to areas with high unemployment to attract new companies.

Diagram 13: Spiral of economic decline

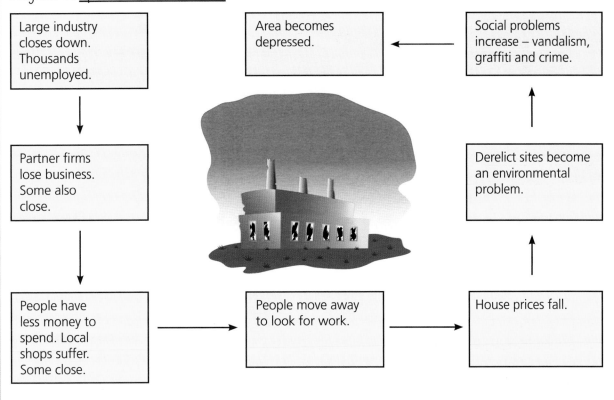

| Large industry closes down. Thousands unemployed. | | Area becomes depressed. | | Social problems increase – vandalism, graffiti and crime. |

| Partner firms lose business. Some also close. | | | | Derelict sites become an environmental problem. |

| People have less money to spend. Local shops suffer. Some close. | | People move away to look for work. | | House prices fall. |

General question 3

Look at the diagram below and on page 47.
Do you think the changes that have taken place between 1974 and 2004 have improved the area?
Give reasons for your answer. **(4 ES marks)**

The Inverfirth Estuary in 1974

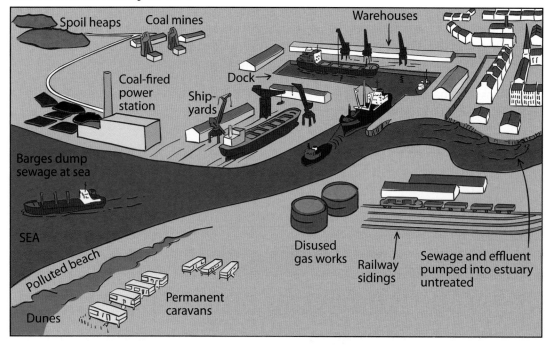

General answer 3

The changes have improved the area a lot. The estuary is a lot cleaner now that sewage is no longer pumped into it (✓) and a proper sewage-treatment works has been built (✓). The beach is much better for visitors because it has been cleaned up (✓) and a car park and picnic site have been provided (✓). Derelict industrial land has been landscaped, making it more attractive (✓), and turned into a country park providing an area for local recreation (✓) which will also help to attract tourists to the area (✓). Jobs lost when industries closed down will have been replaced by new ones in the out-of-town retail park and the waterfront leisure zone (✓).

This answer illustrates how it is important to give reasons to explain why you think the area has improved. Marks are given for explaining how the changes have affected the area, not for describing the changes. You could partly agree and partly disagree, providing that you support your answer with reasons.

General question 4

Look at the diagram below and on page 46.
What techniques could pupils have used to gather the information shown on the diagrams given?
Give reasons for your choice of techniques. **(4 ES marks)**

The Inverfirth Estuary in 2004

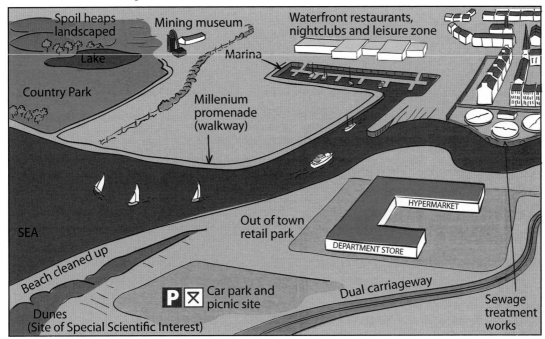

General answer 4

The pupils could have taken pictures of what the area is like now (✓) so that these could be compared with old photos which they might find in the library archive (✓). This would show how the area had changed over the last 30 years (✓). They could also interview older residents (✓), who would be able to describe what buildings there used to be and what the area was like (✓). Looking at old maps would give the pupils an idea of what buildings there were in 1974 (✓). New maps would help them to record how the area had changed since then (✓).

In this 'gathering techniques' question, you must show your knowledge of how geographical data can be collected and match it to the resource you are given. It is important always to explain why the methods you choose would be helpful.

Look out for

When answering about gathering techniques, always say whom you would interview and why, or to which group of people you would give questionnaires and how this data would help the investigation. Never write 'interviewing' or 'questionnaire' without specifying whom you would interview or question!

Credit question 3

The Eden Project – A Visitor Attraction in Cornwall

Study the diagrams below.
Explain fully the advantages **and** disadvantages of this new visitor attraction to St Austell and the surrounding area. **(6 ES marks)**

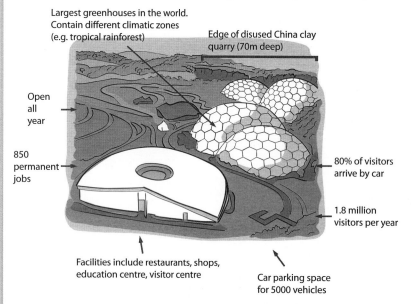

Largest greenhouses in the world. Contain different climatic zones (e.g. tropical rainforest)

Edge of disused China clay quarry (70m deep)

Open all year

850 permanent jobs

80% of visitors arrive by car

1.8 million visitors per year

Facilities include restaurants, shops, education centre, visitor centre

Car parking space for 5000 vehicles

Location of the Eden Project

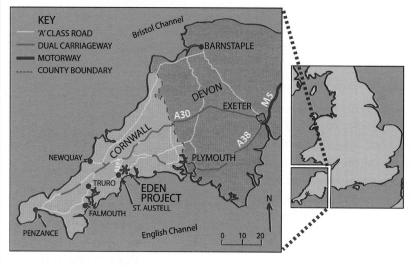

KEY
'A' CLASS ROAD
DUAL CARRIAGEWAY
MOTORWAY
COUNTY BOUNDARY

Bristol Channel

BARNSTAPLE

DEVON

EXETER

M5

A30

CORNWALL

A38

NEWQUAY

PLYMOUTH

TRURO

EDEN PROJECT
ST. AUSTELL

FALMOUTH

PENZANCE

English Channel

N

0 10 20

Credit answer 3

The Eden Project makes good use of an old quarry site which may have been an eyesore (✓). It brings a lot of visitors to the area, which will help the economy (✓), as they will require places to stay and eat, so local businesses will benefit (✓).

The Eden Project itself provides 850 jobs for local people (✓) which are permanent and not just seasonal (✓). It will help to educate local schoolchildren about different environments such as the tropical rainforests (✓). The large number of visitors might cause problems with congestion on the roads (✓), especially as there are only A-class roads which lead to the Eden Project and no dual carriageways (✓). Also, this could cause an increase in air pollution due to the fumes from their exhausts (✓).

The information in the diagrams gives clues to what you should write about; but make sure you do more than just copy the statements. You need to explain fully why a large number of visitors can be both an advantage and a disadvantage, as this answer does. In an 'advantages and disadvantages' question, you must give both to be able to get full marks.

Credit question 4

Llanwern Steelworks, South Wales

Look at the diagram below.

Explain in detail the social, economic and environmental impact of the closure of a large steelworks such as Llanwern on the surrounding area.

(5 KU marks)

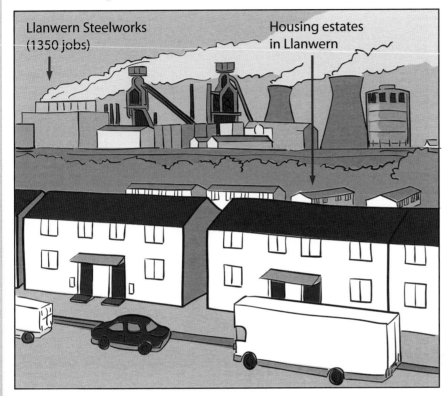

Credit answer 4

Many people will lose their jobs (✓), and other local companies could be affected, resulting in further job losses (✓). As families have less money coming in, they will not be able to spend so much in local shops and restaurants, perhaps causing some of them to shut down too (✓). The site will become derelict and abandoned and may become an environmental problem (✓). To find work, some families will have to move away, causing the area to become further depressed (✓) as school rolls fall and the community dwindles (✓).

This answer makes use of the spiral of economic decline, illustrating how the closure of one major industry can have serious additional consequences for an area. Note that, in order to score full marks, you must try to cover all of the impacts that the question asks about — social, economic and environmental.

KEY IDEA 12

Population is unevenly distributed.

KEY IDEA 13

Populations have measurable social and economic characteristics.

KEY IDEA 14

In any area, the size and structure of the population are subject to change.

Population distribution

What you should know at Credit **level ...**

Population density is the number of people who live in each square kilometre. Areas with a lot of people per square kilometre are **densely populated**; those with few people are **sparsely populated**. The distribution of a country's population is affected by a number of different factors. There are **human factors** which attract population, such as good **accessibility** allowing better trade links. This increases the number of industries, and therefore jobs, as well as the availability of services such as education and health care. Then there are **physical factors** such as the climate, the relief, availability of water supply, the presence of minerals and other raw materials (e.g. coal, timber) and the fertility of the soil which affect people's ability to live in an area.

In most Developed Countries, the vast majority of the population live in urban areas, whereas in Developing Countries it is common to find the majority of the population living in rural areas.

Credit question 1

Population Density of South Island, New Zealand

Look at the diagrams on page 51.

Explain the population distribution on South Island, New Zealand.   **(4 KU marks)**

Population Density of South Island, New Zealand

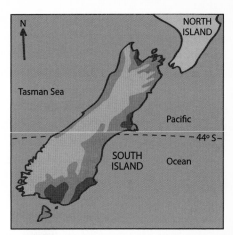

Over 20 persons per square kilometre

2 to 20 persons per square kilometre

0 to 1 person per square kilometre

Relief and Physical Resources

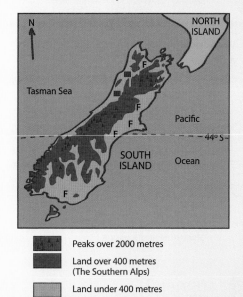

Peaks over 2000 metres

Land over 400 metres
(The Southern Alps)

Land under 400 metres

F   Best farmland

Coalfields

0   500 km

Annual Rainfall

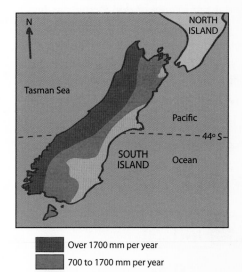

Over 1700 mm per year

700 to 1700 mm per year

Less than 700 mm per year

Credit answer 1

New Zealand's South Island has its most densely populated areas on the eastern and southern coasts. This is because these areas have the best farmland (✓) and the land is lower than in other parts of the island, so the climate will be warmer (✓). The east coast has less rainfall than most other parts of South Island, making it a more favourable area to live in (✓). The west coast of South Island has a low population density because it is very mountainous and therefore difficult to build on (✓) or to create roads and communications (✓). The rainfall levels are also very high, making it an unpleasant part of the island to live in (✓).

In this type of question, it is easy to describe the population density and relate it to the relief or climate. However, this will not achieve any marks unless you also point out what it is that encourages or discourages people to live there. For example, if you say there is a high population density where the land is flatter, this gets no marks because it is just description. If you add that this makes it easier to build settlements, you will get a mark because it is explanation.

Credit question 2

Factors affecting Population Distribution

Which factors, physical **or** human, have the greater influence on population distribution? Give reasons for your choice.   **(6 ES marks)**

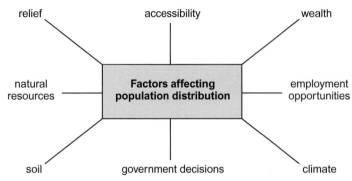

This is an Enquiry Skills question, so there is no mark for choosing physical or human factors. You must make your choice clear and then support it with explanations. Although it is an Enquiry Skills question, a good answer might also include some real-life examples to back up the points you are making.

Sample Credit answer 2

Physical factors are more important, because people usually want to live where the climate is favourable (✔). For this reason, there are more people living in Western Europe, where it is not too hot or dry, than in the Arctic, where it is too cold (✔). Soil is important, because being close to good farmland is vital so that settlements are able to get a food supply easily (✔). The relief of the land has a big influence on where people live because it is much easier to build settlements on flat land than in mountainous areas (✔). The Scottish Highlands have low population density because of this (✔). Many cities have grown where there are natural resources nearby which they can use in industry, so this has a big effect on population density (✔). For example, in Britain, many cities, such as Glasgow, have developed on or close to coalfields (✔).

Measuring population

What you should know at **General** **and** **Credit** **level ...**

A population **census** is when a country's government counts the population and also finds out other information about it. It will find out the **birth rate**, **death rate**, **life expectancy, infant mortality** and many other sorts of information about the people in the country. A census is very expensive to run, and therefore most countries only do it about once a decade. However, the reliability of the information contained in a census depends on how thorough the census has been. Sometimes census data may be unreliable because some parts of a country are inaccessible (sometimes due to war) and not everyone gets counted. There may be **nomadic** people in a country that get missed, or many illiterate people who can neither read nor fill in a form; or some people may be suspicious of the government's motives and fail to give accurate information.

A **population pyramid** shows data about the age structure and sex ratio of a country's population. This is sometimes known as the **population structure**. You should be able to recognise the differences in the shapes of the population pyramids of developed and developing countries and be able to give reasons for these differences.

You also need to know why differences exist in key population data between developed and developing countries. For example, why are birth rates lower in Britain than in, say, Nigeria? Or, why is life expectancy lower in Uganda than in Germany?

General question 1

Population Data – India

Look at the table below.

'In an Economically Less Developed Country such as India, the population figures taken from census records are likely to be unreliable.' – UN spokesperson

Do you agree with the above statement?

Give reasons for your answer. **(3 ES marks)**

Year	Population in Millions
1945	336
1955	395
1965	482
1975	600
1985	749
1995	934
2005	1095

General answer 1

Yes, I agree that census data in developing countries might be unreliable because they may not be able to afford to carry out the census fully (✓), and people in remote parts of the country may be missed out if these are inaccessible (✓). In some countries, there may be nomadic people who are missed out because they are out of the country during the census (✓). The data in India could become unreliable quickly if there is a high birth or death rate (✓), or if there is a lot of immigration (✓).

Although this answer agrees with the statement all the way through, your answer could partly agree and partly disagree. The key thing is to make sure that you give clear reasons for your choice.

Look out for

Rich or **developed countries** may be known as **economically more developed countries** (**EMDCs**), while poorer or **developing countries** may be known as **economically less developed countries** (**ELDCs**). In exams before 2010, the terms ELDC and EMDC were used in many exam questions.

General question 2

Population Data – India

Look at the table below.
What other techniques could be used to show the information in the table?
Explain your choice(s). **(4 ES marks)**

Year	Population in Millions
1945	336
1955	395
1965	482
1975	600
1985	749
1995	934
2005	1095

General answer 2

The census data could be shown as a line graph (✔). This would be suitable, because line graphs show changes over time well (✔). It could be used to make quite accurate estimates of the population in years between each census (✔).

A bar graph could also be used (✔). The bar graph would show the rising trend in the population (✔).

In processing techniques questions where there is more than one set of data, make sure that you specify clearly which data set your chosen technique is referring to.

This is a four-mark 'processing techniques' question. To score full marks, you must give at least two valid techniques and also reasons to explain why they would be suitable. You will always be expected to give more than one technique to be able to gain full marks.

General question 3

Population Data for two Countries

Which set of population data, A or B, is more typical of an Economically Less Developed Country (ELDC)? Give reasons for your choice. **(4 KU marks)**

Population Data A

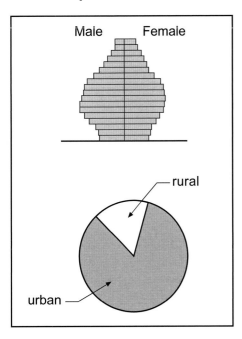

Population Data B

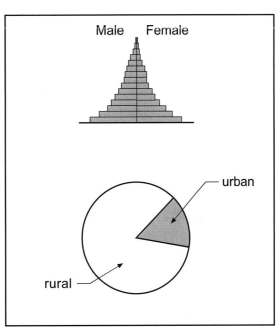

General answer 3

B shows the economically less developed country (✓). This is because the population pyramid shows that there are a lot of children born, which is typical of many developing-world countries (✓), and that there are few older people (✓). This could be because health care is poor or unavailable (✓). Also, there are more people living in the countryside than in the city, which is true for many ELDCs (✓).

This is a Knowledge question, and there is a mark given for choosing the correct set of data. To gain the other three marks, you have to show your knowledge of population pyramids and of the differences in population structure between developing and developed countries.

Credit question 3

Look at the diagrams below.
Give reasons why it may be difficult to take an accurate census in **a developing** counry such as Bolivia. **(5 KU marks)**

Location of Bolivia

Bolivia

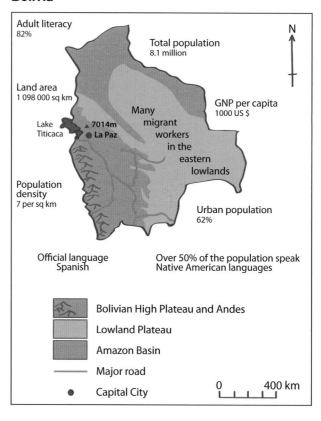

Adult literacy
82%

Total population
8.1 million

Land area
1 098 000 sq km

GNP per capita
1000 US $

Lake Titicaca

▲ 7014m

● La Paz

Many migrant workers in the eastern lowlands

Population density
7 per sq km

Urban population
62%

Official language
Spanish

Over 50% of the population speak Native American languages

Bolivian High Plateau and Andes

Lowland Plateau

Amazon Basin

— Major road

● Capital City

0   400 km

Credit answer 3

There may be many physical obstacles, such as mountain ranges, which stop census workers from reaching every part of the country (✓). There may be tribes in the Amazon rainforest which cannot be reached (✓). Even if they could be, there would be language barriers and they might not understand the forms (✓). As the official language is Spanish, and 50% of the population speak different languages, there will be a language problem across the country (✓). Also, people in many parts of Bolivia may be illiterate and so unable to fill in the forms (✓). There are many migrant workers in the eastern lowlands, and some of them might be there illegally, so they would not want to fill in the form at all (✓).

The information on the diagram is there to help you. Although you will not get marks for copying statements from the diagram, this answer uses some of the information and develops it further into a valid point. Sometimes you will gain two marks for one idea if it is fully explained and becomes a 'developed point'.

This answer mentions the problem of language barriers but explains it in detail using information from the diagram, and so gains two marks.

Credit question 4

Bolivia

What use could a Government of **a developing** country make of population census data?   **(4 KU marks)**

Credit answer 4

The government in a developing country could use the information from a census to plan services for the population (✓). If there are a lot of births, it could spend money on educating people more about birth control (✓) and on clinics for mothers and young children (✓). This might help to bring about reductions in the birth rate and in infant mortality (✓). The census would allow the government to see where the greatest number of children were and spend more money on schools in those areas (✓). Finally, it could work out how much tax it could collect if it knew exactly how many people were in the country (✓).

This Knowledge and Understanding question is worth four marks. The answer makes five valid points about how the government might use census data. It is always a good idea to make at least one more point than there are marks available – the examiners might not agree with every point you make!

Credit question 5

Population Pyramids for New Zealand and Indonesia

Look at the diagrams below.

'New Zealand is a developed country and Indonesia is a developing country.'

Give reasons for the differences between the population structures of New Zealand and Indonesia.   **(6 KU marks)**

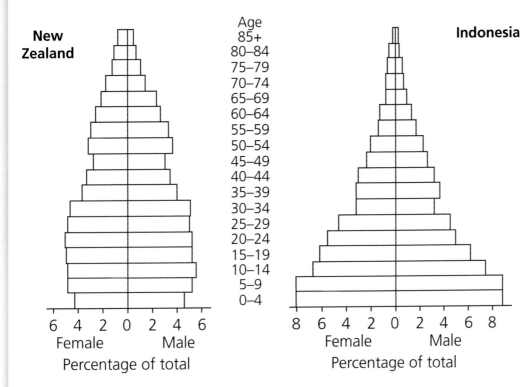

Credit answer 5

Indonesia has a much higher birth rate than New Zealand because the former is a developing-world country and may not be able to afford the same amount of education about family planning (✓). Families in Indonesia may have more children because they need to send them out to work at a young age to earn money (✓) or to make sure that there are still some children left to look after the parents when they reach old age (✓). In New Zealand, families won't need to worry about this because they can afford better pensions and care for the elderly (✓). There are far more old people in New Zealand because it has a higher standard of living than Indonesia (✓), and there will be better health care too, so that fewer people die of diseases which can be cured (✓). In Indonesia, but not in New Zealand, there will be shanty towns, where diseases spread quickly causing life expectancy to be lower there (✓).

Notice how every statement in this answer gives a reason for a difference shown on the population pyramid. Without this explanation, the answer is just description and would get no marks. It is not necessary to explain every difference on the population pyramids, so long as you make sufficient points to score full marks. Always try to give different reasons, as you will not get another mark if you give the same reasons for each difference.

Population change

What you should know at **General** **and** **Credit** **level ...**

You need to learn about how and why populations change. This could be due to **immigration** or **emigration** or a combination of the two. Changes in the **birth rate** and **death rate** can be caused by natural factors such as famine and epidemics, or by human factors such as birth control or better health care.

You should learn why people might decide to migrate. Often, this is to seek better jobs and housing, higher pay and a better standard of living, but it may sometimes be because people have become **refugees** due to a war or natural disaster and need somewhere else to live. In particular, you will be expected to be able to give reasons for rural–urban migration in developing-world countries and how this can lead to the formation of **shanty towns.** Often, life in these shanty towns might be worse than what people have left behind in the countryside, but the prospect of being able to get a better job or higher wages keeps drawing people in.

Some questions will ask you about changing populations over a longer period of time, and you may be asked to look at a diagram of the **demographic transition model** (see page 61, Credit question 6). So long as you can explain why birth and death rates were high or low at any particular point on the graph, and what might have caused them to change, you should be able to do well on this topic.

General question 4

Population Structure in Hungary

Look at the diagrams below.

Describe the changes which are expected to take place in the population structure of Hungary by 2049. **(3 ES marks)**

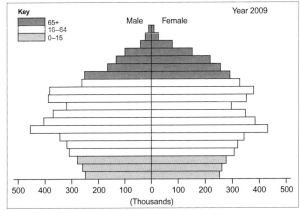

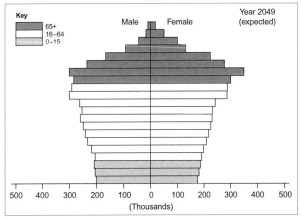

General answer 4

By 2049, there will be fewer babies being born (✓) and there will be fewer young people aged around 20 to 30 (✓). There will be far more old people aged 65 or over (✓), and the life expectancy will have gone up (✓).

This is a 'describe' question, and there is no need to give explanations. Simple statements pointing out the differences are all that is required. Where possible, make your answer more precise and detailed by referring to data from the graph.

General question 5

Population Structure in Hungary

Look at the diagrams below.

What problems might the expected population structure in 2049 create for Hungary? **(4 KU marks)**

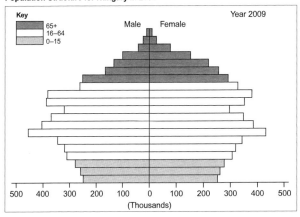

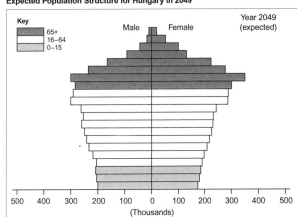

General answer 5

If there are fewer babies being born, there will be fewer children in schools, and so some may have to close down (✓). Fewer young people could mean that Hungary will not have enough workers (✓), and this could cause the country's economy to suffer (✓). More old people will require more money to be spent on pensions (✓), and the government will need to spend more money on care for the elderly (✓). With fewer workers and more old people, the government will have to put up taxes (✓).

Make sure, in this type of question, that you state clearly what the problem is. Fewer children in schools is not necessarily a problem, but, if this results in the closure of schools, it is a problem for the communities involved. Any change which involves an increase in government spending is a potential problem for that country.

General question 6

Factors which influence Death Rates in Europe

Look at the diagram below.

For any **two** of the factors shown, **explain** how they affect death rates in Europe.   **(4 KU marks)**

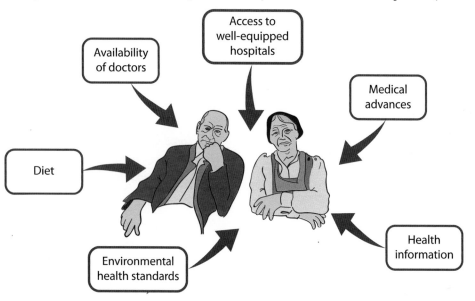

General answer 6

Availability of doctors: there is good access to doctors in Europe, and so this will help to keep death rates down (✓) because, if people fall ill, they will have a good chance of being seen by a doctor and being cured (✓), whereas in the developing world people with the same illness may not have access to doctors and could die more easily (✓).

Health information: there is good access to information about how to stay healthy, and this will keep death rates down (✓). For example, people are told not to smoke and to get plenty of exercise, so this will help to stop people from falling ill (✓).

In this question, you must explain how your chosen factors affect the death rate in Europe. Not all of the factors will necessarily keep death rates low. For example, you could argue that poor diet (too much sugar and fatty food) could increase the death rate.

Credit question 6

Demographic Transition Model

Look at the graph below.

Describe in detail the changes shown on the Demographic Transition Model from Stage 1 to Stage 4.   **(4 ES marks)**

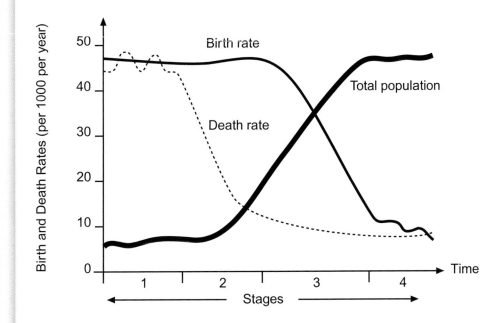

Credit answer 6

In stage 1, the birth and death rate are both high but the death rate goes up and down more (✓). In stage 2, the birth rate stays high but the death rate drops quickly (✓), from over 40 to about 12 per 1000 per year (✓).

In stage 3, the birth rate starts to drop fast (✓) while the death rate only drops gradually (✓). In stage 4, the birth rate is still falling but more gradually (✓).

Although this question only asks you to describe the changes, you should also learn about reasons for the changes to the birth and death rates shown. You should be prepared to explain why the changes on the demographic transition model have happened.

*It is important to notice that you only need to describe the changes on the graph to score full marks in this question. There is no need for explanations, as they will not gain any marks. Notice too that marks are only given for changes, so the opening statement about the birth and death rates being high does not gain a mark because it has not described a change. The mark is given at the end for describing the death rate going up and down – this is a **change**. Use figures from the graph to make your answer detailed. Also, you do not have to describe everything on the graph, so long as you make enough valid statements to secure full marks (this answer, for example, does not mention the total population).*

Credit question 7

Selected Population Data

Look at the table below.

Choose **one** country shown on the table.

Suggest reasons for its **rate of natural increase**.   (4 KU marks)

Country	Crude Birth Rate per 1000	Crude Death Rate per 1000	Natural Increase per 1000
India	23	8	15
Nigeria	38	14	24
UK	10·8	10·1	0·7
USA	14·1	8·3	5·8

Credit answer 7

In Nigeria, the natural increase is quite high at 24. This is because there is a high birth rate (✓), which could be because couples want to have plenty of children so that some can be sent out to earn money for the family (✓), or because they are worried that not all of their children will live to adulthood (✓), as infant mortality is often quite high in African countries (✓). The parents may also want children to look after them when they are older and no longer able to work (✓). The death rate may have fallen in recent years due to improvements in health care (✓).

This is a Knowledge question, where you are expected to show that you know why populations in some countries are rising quickly. This could be due to a combination of high birth rates and medical advances causing the death rates to fall.

Look out for

Population growth rate, also known as the natural increase, is the difference between the birth rate and the death rate.

International relations are dominated by a limited number of countries acting in conjunction with others.

Regions of the world are linked through trade.

Schemes of self-help, along with national and international aid, seek to encourage social and economic development.

International relations

What you should know at **General** and **Credit** level ...

Certain countries or groups of countries dominate international relations and trade because they control large amounts of resources, because of their size and population or because of their historical development and their level of technology. China is clearly a country with growing international importance, but in Standard Grade papers, examples will refer to Europe, the USA or Japan.

You will be expected to know how, because of their wealth and economic power, the European Union (EU), Japan and the USA control a disproportionately high percentage of world trade. They can exert a lot of pressure on less powerful countries to lower the price of their exports. Often, trade barriers, in the form of import taxes called **tariffs**, are created to make it more difficult for smaller countries to export their goods to these more wealthy nations. For example, the EU imposes tariffs on food produced by other countries, which producers within the EU do not have to pay. You should know about the ideas behind **fair trade**, and the advantages of this for producers in smaller countries.

You should know about the advantages for countries of membership of an alliance such as the EU. A country joining the EU will benefit, for example, from a huge market in excess of 300 million people and free trade within it, a higher political status in world affairs and greater national security in having a large group of allies.

General question 1

Selected World Oil Consumption, 2005

Look at the diagram below.

Explain why certain areas such as the USA, Europe and Japan use such a great amount of the world's oil.   **(4 KU marks)**

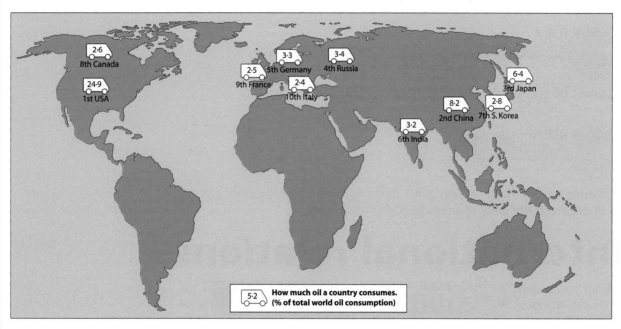

General answer 1

Areas such as the USA, Europe and Japan use such a large amount of the world's oil because they have a lot of industry and so use a lot of energy (✓). Also, their large populations have a high standard of living, which requires a lot of fuel supplies (✓) because many families run two cars which all need oil (✓), and their houses are centrally heated, many by oil (✓). Poorer countries in Africa, for example, don't require anything like as much energy because they have less industry (✓).

In this Knowledge question, you must show that you understand why the USA, Europe and Japan consume so much oil. Any references to aspects of the economy and lifestyle in these countries which show that they are energy-hungry will gain credit. Also, comparison with the lower need for energy in less affluent countries shows good knowledge.

General question 2

Maize Trade between USA and Mexico

'Farmers in poor countries must be given a fair chance to compete, both in world markets and at home.' – Kofi Annan (United Nations General Secretary)

Look at the diagram below.

Explain why Mexican farmers think the maize trade between the USA and their country is unfair. **(4 KU marks)**

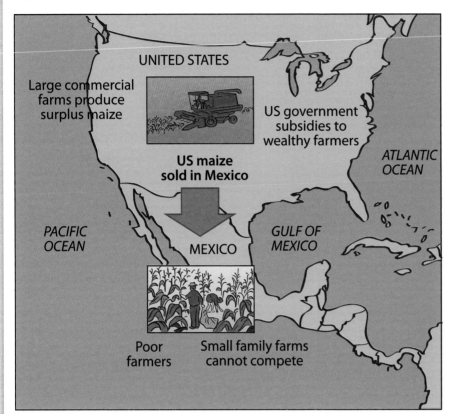

General answer 2

Farmers in the USA have large farms with lots of machinery such as combine harvesters producing large amounts of maize (✓), whereas Mexican farms are small and cannot compete with this (✓). American farmers also receive government subsidies, while Mexican farmers don't (✓). Mexican farmers are poor and can't afford to invest in their farms, whereas American farmers are wealthy (✓). The surplus maize imported from the USA into Mexico will swamp the market, making it much more difficult for Mexican farmers to sell their maize (✓).

In this Enquiry Skills question, there is a lot of information on the diagram which can be used in your answer. You have to make sure that the information you select from the diagram is used in a way that answers the question properly. It is not enough just to copy the information from the diagram; you are required to show that you can use it in a relevant way.

General question 3

Headquarters of the World's 100 Largest Companies

Look at the diagram below.

Give reasons for the location of the world's largest companies.   **(3 KU marks)**

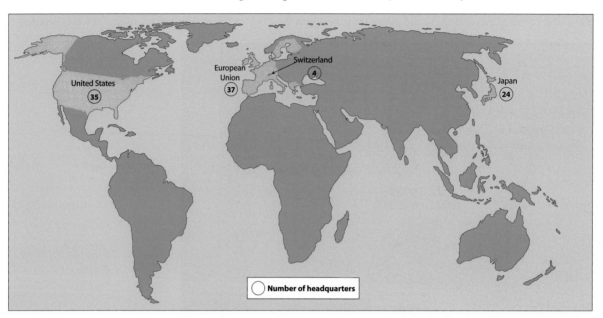

European Union ⓷⓻

Switzerland ④

United States ㉟

Japan ㉔

◯ **Number of headquarters**

General answer 3

The diagram shows that the headquarters of the world's 100 largest companies are all in the USA, Japan or countries in Europe. This is because these are the wealthiest countries in the world, and the companies' owners come from there (✓). Most of their business will be done within these parts of the world, so it is convenient to locate their HQs there (✓). The companies will have developed in the USA, Europe or Japan and so have always been there (✓). It would not be as efficient if they had their HQ in a part of the world which was far away from most of their customers (✓).

In this question, you have to show your knowledge of why these countries tend to dominate world trade. This is due to their wealth and the high standard of living in the USA, Japan and Europe, which requires a lot of trade to keep it going. These countries may in the past have exploited resources from other parts of the world to generate their wealth and may still do so today.

Credit question 1

Location of the 10 new Members of the European Union

The European Union has been enlarged from its previous membership of 15 countries to a group of 25.
Explain the economic and political advantages to the 10 new countries of joining the European Union.   **(5 KU marks)**

- ESTONIA
- LATVIA
- LITHUANIA
- POLAND
- CZECH REPUBLIC
- SLOVAKIA
- HUNGARY
- SLOVENIA
- MALTA
- CYPRUS

■ 15 members of EU before enlargement
□ New member states

500 km

Credit answer 1

The ten new countries joined the EU because they will benefit from being part of the huge single market with over 200 million customers (✓), and they will not have to pay import taxes (tariffs) to sell their products, as they are now part of the EU (✓). The people in these countries will be able to move to any other country within the EU to seek work (✓). They will benefit from having more bargaining power in their trading relationships with the rest of the world (✓). By joining the EU, the new countries might have the chance to become part of the Euro zone (✓), and they will have new allies who could come to their aid if they were threatened by another country (✓).

To score full marks in this question, you have to mention both economic and political benefits. Knowledge of the advantages of EU membership will help you to answer this type of question – for example, how tariffs work in favour of countries which are members.

Look out for

Leave a gap of two or three lines between each of your Credit answers so that, if you have time at the end, or if you remember something you've missed later on in the exam, you will have space to go back and add it in.

Credit question 2

Japan's Exports

Look at the diagrams below.

Japan has a large trade surplus and is the world's second biggest trading nation.
Explain why Japan depends on world trade for the success of its economy.   **(3 KU marks)**

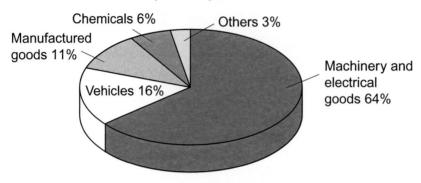

Japan's Exports

- Chemicals 6%
- Others 3%
- Manufactured goods 11%
- Vehicles 16%
- Machinery and electrical goods 64%

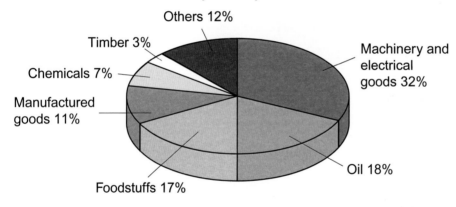

Japan's Imports

- Others 12%
- Timber 3%
- Chemicals 7%
- Manufactured goods 11%
- Machinery and electrical goods 32%
- Oil 18%
- Foodstuffs 17%

Credit answer 2

Japan trades very successfully with the rest of the world because it buys a lot of raw materials and resources from other parts of the world and sells manufactured products such as machinery, electrical goods and cars to the rest of the world (✔). It will buy the raw materials for a low price from developing-world countries and sell its manufactured products at a high price, making a healthy profit (✔). If it didn't trade so much with the rest of the world, it would not be able to produce so many manufactured goods, as it doesn't have enough raw materials of its own (✔), and its own population would be too small to buy up all the products, so it is very dependent on world trade (✔).

Japan is typical of a rich country in the developed world which buys raw materials from developing-world countries and manufactures expensive products from them which it then sells on. Some of this information can be gained by studying the two pie charts, but you are expected to show some knowledge of the way in which countries like Japan dominate world trade.

World trade

What you should know at **General** **and** **Credit** **level ...**

You must learn the meaning of terms such as **imports**, **exports** and the **balance of trade**. When a country imports goods worth more than the value of its exports, it is said to have a **trade deficit**. When the value of its exports is greater than the amount it spends on imports, then it is said to have a **trade surplus**. A large trade surplus is good for a country because it means that there will be money for investment, higher wages and a healthy economy.

You should know about the ways in which many countries in the developing world are exploited by developed countries that will buy their raw materials at very low prices. Often, developing-world countries have only a few different types of goods to sell, so that, if the price of one commodity falls, that country's economy can be hit very badly. For example, the Ivory Coast is the world's largest producer and exporter of cocoa beans, and it is heavily dependent on exporting cocoa beans at a good price. If the price of cocoa beans on the world market falls, the Ivory Coast will be badly affected. Its farmers and their families can lose a large part of their income, resulting in poverty and suffering. The Ivory Coast now has a growing oil industry, and this helps it to have another source of income if the prices of agricultural products such as cocoa beans fall. A country with a good variety of different exports is better placed to ride out fluctuations in world commodity prices.

General question 4

United States – Imports and Exports (2000–2005 Average)

Look at the diagrams below.

Give **other** processing techniques which could be used to show the information in the diagram below. Why are these techniques suitable? **(4 ES marks)**

% Imports

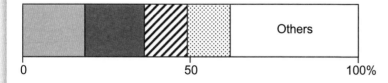

0   50   100%

% Exports

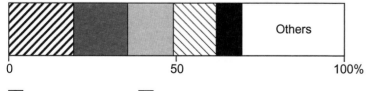

0   50   100%

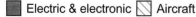

▢ Vehicles	▢ Fuels
▢ Electric & electronic	▢ Aircraft
▢ Nuclear equipment	▢ Scientific equipment

General answer 4

The information on imports and exports could also be shown on two pie charts (✓). This is because the data is already given in percentages, which makes it easy to convert into pie charts (✓). Each segment of the pie chart can be colour-coded to represent a particular commodity (✓). The two pie charts, side by side, will allow clear comparisons to be made (✓).

The information could also be shown in a table with two columns, one for exports and one for imports (✓). The data could be put in rank order, with the largest exports and imports first (✓) so that it would be easy to see the differences.

In this 'processing techniques' question, you must give at least two valid techniques and explain why they are suitable. Note that the answer specifies two pie charts, one for imports and one for exports. One pie chart on its own could not show all of this information. You must always be careful to link the technique you are using to the data in the diagram. Sometimes one technique might only be suitable for part of the information, but this is OK so long as you say which information you are referring to. In this question, other techniques which are suitable include a bar graph and a pictogram.

Credit question 3

Exports of selected Economically Less Developed Countries (Developing Countries)

Look at the diagram below.

Explain why some Economically Less Developed Countries (Developing Countries) are especially at risk from changing world prices for the goods which they export. **(4 KU marks)**

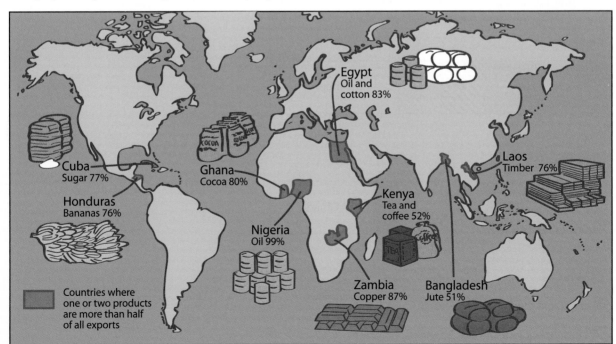

Credit answer 3

Developing-world countries may be especially at risk from changing world prices for their goods, because they are over-dependent on one or two products for most of their income (✓). For example, Zambia depends on copper for 87% of its income, so, if world copper prices fall a lot, the country will have very little else that it can sell (✓), and its economy could go into a sharp decline (✓). This could result in copper miners being laid off and their families facing hardship because they will have lost their main source of income (✓). If they had a good range of other exports, their economy would be better able to survive the falls in world commodity prices (✓).

Many developing-world countries depend on their exports of just a few raw materials and are vulnerable to fluctuations in world prices. This answer uses an example from the diagram to back up the previous statement. To score full marks on this question, you need to show that you know about the risks of having just one or two main exports as well as the economic and social consequences that can result from this.

Look out for

If the question is for, say, five marks, always try to make at least six points in your answer. Use the number of marks as a rough guide to how much to write in your answer.

Credit question 4

Exports of selected Economically Less Developed Countries (Developing Countries)

Look at the diagram below.
Which other processing techniques could be used to display the export percentage figures shown.
Give reasons for your choice of tecniques.   **(6 ES marks)**

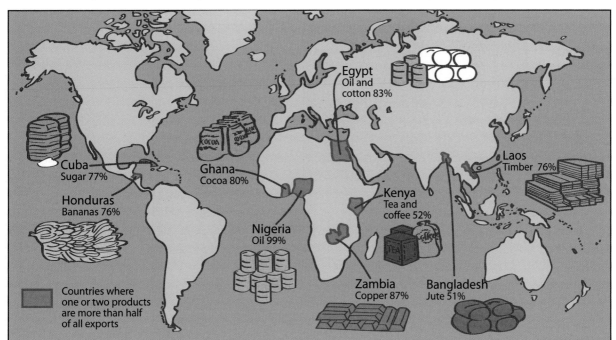

Credit answer 4

These export figures could be shown in a series of pie charts (✓), as they are already in percentages (✓). The pie charts could be viewed in a row to allow comparison of countries (✓).

The information could also be shown in a bar graph (✓), with each bar representing a different country's dependence on one major export (✓). The bars could be ranked from largest to smallest to show that Nigeria is the most dependent on one export (✓).

A table displaying the information as a list could also be used (✓).

For each technique that you choose, you should always try to back it up with one or two reasons. Give different reasons for each technique, because you will not get repeat marks for the same reason. This Credit 'techniques' question differs from a General one (see General question 4 above) in that it is worth more marks and you are expected to give more techniques and/or reasons.

Look out for

In 'processing techniques' questions, make sure that you specify whether one pie chart or bar chart is adequate or whether the data would need to be displayed in a series of two or more pie charts or bar charts. This will depend on how many different sets of data there are in the question.

Credit question 5

Location of the Three Gorges Dam

The Three Gorges Dam project was built with money from China and investments from Japan, Canada, Germany and Switzerland. These investments were made in order to develop trade with China.

What are the advantages **and** disadvantages for China and its trading partners of using these investments to build the Three Gorges Dam? **(6 ES marks)**

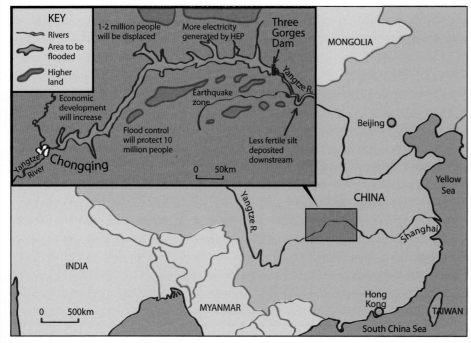

Credit answer 5

China will get many benefits from this investment. It will get a large supply of renewable energy, which is helping the environment by keeping carbon emissions low (✓). China's economy will also benefit from this new power source (✓), and, if the economy is successful, its trading partners will get a good return from their investment too (✓). On the other hand, the dam is in an earthquake zone, and this could result in catastrophe if the dam is breached (✓). Also, 1.2 million people have been displaced in order to create the reservoir, and many of them will not be happy (✓). Fertile silt which previously would have been deposited in the flood plain downstream from the Three Gorges will now be trapped behind the dam, resulting in the need for more chemical fertilisers on farmland (✓). Also, the silt will need to be dredged out from the reservoir, and this will be expensive (✓).

In this type of question, you must ensure that your answer gives both advantages and disadvantages, because you will not get full marks if you don't. The statements around the diagram are there as prompts, and you should use them to help you explain the good and bad points about this development. However, you must do more than just copy these statements, as this will reduce the number of marks you can get. Any relevant knowledge that you can add to your answer (such as the environmental advantages of hydro-electric power) will also help to gain marks.

Aid

What you should know at **General** **and** **Credit** **level ...**

There are three main types of aid. These are **charitable** or **voluntary aid**, which is collected by charities such as Oxfam or the Red Cross; **bilateral** (or **tied**) **aid**, which is given by one (usually wealthy country) to another (usually developing country) but often with conditions linked to it; and **multilateral aid**, which is given by a group of countries such as the United Nations or the European Union to a developing-world country. You should know each type of aid and be able to state its main advantages and disadvantages.

Self-help schemes are popular ways of making use of aid money in developing-world countries. With just a small amount of money, groups of people in these countries can learn skills which they can then pass on to others. So, if the money runs out, they are still able to use their skills for the benefit of the community. For example, a small of amount of money (several thousand pounds) was used to teach building skills to young people in the Tanzanian town of Arusha. They were then able to construct useful buildings for their community, such as medical centres and schools, as well as to train other young people to gain the skills they needed to be able to get jobs. Often, this type of aid appears to be more beneficial to the community than large-scale aid schemes.

Short–term aid is used to help countries which have been hit by disasters such as earthquakes or famines. This involves getting emergency supplies such as food, shelter and medicines to the victims quickly in order to save their lives and reduce their suffering. **Long-term aid** is used for projects that might not be needed immediately but will help the community in the long run. For example, a programme of building more schools will help the literacy rate in a country and eventually help the country to develop as more people are trained and have the skills to take on jobs which will help the country.

General question 5

Self-help Schemes

Look at the diagrams below.
Why are self-help schemes suitable for Economically Less Developed Countries (ELDCs)?   **(3 KU marks)**

Improved plough

Hand pump

Stone lines

General answer 5

Self-help schemes are suitable for developing countries because often they are small-scale projects which help local communities (✓). They usually only require a modest amount of money (✓) and provide something useful to people such as a clean water supply (✓). In some projects, people learn skills (✓), which they can continue to use all their lives (✓).

This is a Knowledge question, where you must show that you know about self-help schemes. The information in the diagrams can be used as examples, but you will need to bring your own knowledge into this type of question to be able to gain full marks.

Look out for

Stone lines placed along the contours of the land are an effective way of preventing soil erosion and are often used to help stop desertification. These 'magic stones' are an example of a self-help scheme.

General question 6

Tied Aid

Look at the diagram below.
What are the advantages and disadvantages of tied aid for ELDCs?　　　(4 ES marks)

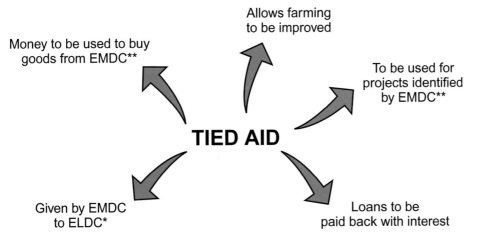

Money to be used to buy
goods from EMDC**

Allows farming
to be improved

To be used for
projects identified
by EMDC**

TIED AID

Given by EMDC
to ELDC*

Loans to be
paid back with interest

*ELDC　=　Economically Less Developed Country
**EMDC　=　Economically More Developed Country

General answer 6

Tied aid is good for developing countries because they can get a lot of money for major projects such as building a dam (✓). It helps to establish links with the donor country in the developed world (✓). However, the aid often comes with conditions attached, which might not benefit the developing country (✓). For example, they will often have to pay back loans with large amounts of interest (✓), which can lead the country into debt (✓).

Bilateral or tied aid is given from one country to another, but there are often strings attached. To gain full marks in this question, you should give at least two advantages and two disadvantages, as the question asks for more than one of each. In this Enquiry Skills question, there is a lot of information in the diagram which you can use.

General question 7

Effects of Asian Tsunami, December 2004

'Immediate help is essential but we also need long term aid for a full recovery.' – Government spokesperson

For this type of natural disaster, **describe** what could be done to help these areas **in the longer term.** (4 KU marks)

Damage in Nam Khem village, Thailand

Devastation at Petang beach resort, Thailand

Farmland destroyed, Sri Lanka

General answer 7

In the long term, these communities will need help for rebuilding (✓). Bridges may have been destroyed and will need to be rebuilt (✓) so that transport can get back up and running (✓). In some places, it may be necessary to reconstruct people's homes further back from the coast (✓). Fields that were destroyed will need to be drained and repaired (✓) so that these communities can grow their own food again (✓).

Long-term aid is required after the initial short-term needs of the victims have been seen to. For example, medical help and temporary shelters, including tents and blankets, may all be needed in the short term, but afterwards long-term aid is needed for rebuilding, so that these communities can once again become viable.

Credit question 6

Different types of Aid in ELDCs

'Aid from charities is better than bilateral aid.'

Do you agree fully with this statement?

Give reasons for your answer.   **(4 ES marks)**

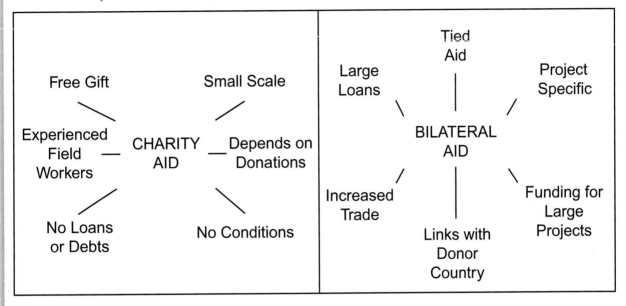

Credit answer 6

I partly agree with this statement. Charity aid is good because it doesn't usually have conditions linked to it, whereas bilateral aid does (✓), which could involve the country being forced into debt when it has to repay loans (✓). Charities often send out experienced field workers to help set up the aid project, and this is an extra benefit for the developing country (✓). On the other hand, bilateral aid could be better because it usually gives larger sums of money (✓) which will allow much bigger projects to take place (✓).

This question asks you whether you agree fully with the statement. It allows you to partly agree and to partly disagree. This usually gives more scope for an answer than having to argue all one way. It is therefore often easier to phrase your answer like the response here, which has selected the advantages of each type of aid from the two diagrams.

Organised events to which you have contributed, such as Children in Need or Sport Relief, are involved in many charitable aid schemes in developing countries. Quoting examples you know about will help you gain marks, if they are relevant to the question.

Credit question 7

Mount Nyiragongo erupts, 17 January 2002

Look at the diagrams below.

Following the eruption of Mount Nyiragongo, aid was rushed to the area.

Which type of aid would be best suited to helping the people of this area following the volcanic eruption?

Give reasons for your answer.　　**(5 ES marks)**

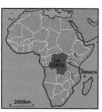

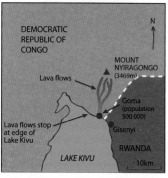

- dozens killed
- crops and farmland destroyed
- lava flows sweep through 14 villages, setting fire to fuel and power stations
- Goma Airport runway blocked by lava
- water supplies cut off
- 10 000 people made homeless
- harbour facilities on Lake Kivu destroyed

Short Term Aid	Long Term Aid
Tents and blankets	Road and bridge repairs
Medicines	New house building
Food supplies	Farming equipment and fertilisers

Credit answer 7

Short-term aid would be best because there are a lot of things which need to be done immediately. For example, the water supplies were cut off, and people would need water straight away (✓). Medical aid would have to be rushed in, as there may have been injured people needing treatment (✓), and with refugees all crowded together there would be a danger that disease could spread quickly (✓). People were made homeless, and so they would need emergency shelters (✓). Crops and farmland were destroyed, so people would have lost their main source of food and would require food supplies quickly (✓), otherwise there could be problems with malnutrition or starvation (✓).

The diagrams contain information which could be used in support of either short-term or long-term aid. In this Enquiry Skills question, you need to select the relevant information and show how it supports your choice. You can also add any relevant knowledge which you have on this topic. After major disasters such as earthquakes or, in this case, a volcanic eruption, short-term aid will always be required to assist casualties and provide services for victims who have lost their homes. Short-term aid is therefore a good choice for answering this question.

Short-term aid is often known as **emergency aid.**

Aid is usually the last question in the exam. Write as detailed an answer as you can, and, if you have time left, go back and see if you can add a sentence to other answers earlier in the paper. It could make the difference between achieving a higher grade or just missing out.

Answering map questions

What you should know at General **and** Credit **level ...**

Map questions account for approximately one third of the marks at Standard Grade. In General papers, you can expect about 23 or 24 marks (out of 70) to be map-based questions, while at Credit level there are usually 26 or 27 marks (out of 80) on map questions, so it is essential that you have lots of practice at map work throughout your course. Similar questions can appear on General and on Credit maps, but the Credit questions are usually worth more marks. It is worth noting, too, that you should spend approximately one third of your time in the exam answering the map questions (about 25 to 30 minutes at General and about 40 minutes at Credit level).

There is often a reference diagram printed on the question papers to direct you to certain parts of the Ordnance Survey map extract. You must use this in conjunction with the map extract to answer the questions. Never try to answer the questions without looking carefully at the map extract.

Examiners will be looking for evidence that you have read and correctly interpreted the map, so it is a good idea to use grid references to identify places on the map to which you are referring. You will often receive an extra mark the first time that you correctly use an appropriate grid reference. As with other sections of the course, you will be expected to give more detailed responses at Credit than at General level.

Physical map questions

What you should know at General **and** Credit **level ...**

Map extracts are often chosen to show good examples of physical features which you will have learned about during your course. These include glacial and river landscapes. You must be able to identify on a map the main features of a landscape of glacial erosion and of a river and its valley. In a glaciated area, these could include U-shaped valleys, arêtes, corries, ribbon lochs, pyramidal peaks, truncated spurs and hanging valleys. Along a river and its valley, features might include meanders, oxbow lakes, tributaries, confluences, waterfalls, river islands (eyots), braiding and flood plains. You might be able to comment on the width and depth of the valley, whether the river is in its upper, middle or lower course and whether the section of river appearing on the map is tidal or not (shown by a black instead of a blue outline to the river).

On physical maps too, there are often questions relating to land use and land-use conflicts. Forestry is a common topic on physical maps, and you should know what factors make an area suitable for a commercial forestry plantation. Also, you should be able to identify possible land-use conflicts in a rural area, say between farming and hillwalkers. Remember, the key to giving a good map answer is always to use map evidence. Don't give vague generalised answers!

Diagram 14: _Glacial features on Ordnance Survey maps_

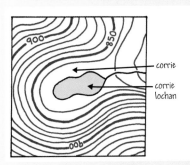
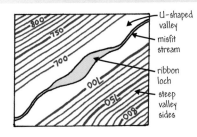
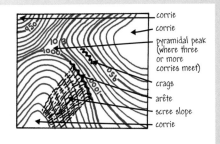

Diagram 15: <u>Selected Ordnance Survey 1:50,000 Map Symbols</u>

General Information

LAND FEATURES

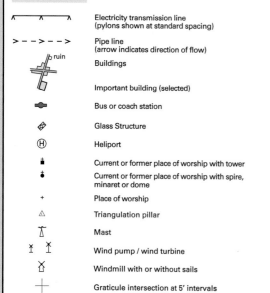

Electricity transmission line
(pylons shown at standard spacing)

Pipe line
(arrow indicates direction of flow)

Buildings

Important building (selected)

Bus or coach station

Glass Structure

Heliport

Current or former place of worship with tower

Current or former place of worship with spire, minaret or dome

Place of worship

Triangulation pillar

Mast

Wind pump / wind turbine

Windmill with or without sails

Graticule intersection at 5' intervals

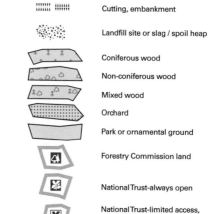

Cutting, embankment

Landfill site or slag / spoil heap

Coniferous wood

Non-coniferous wood

Mixed wood

Orchard

Park or ornamental ground

Forestry Commission land

National Trust-always open

National Trust-limited access, observe local signs

National Trust for Scotland - always open

National Trust for Scotland - limited access, observe local signs

HEIGHTS

50 Contours are at 10 metres vertical interval

· 144 Heights are to the nearest metre above mean sea level

Where two heights are shown, the first height is to the base of the triangulation pillar and the second (in brackets) to the highest natural point of the hill

ABBREVIATIONS

More information on abbreviations and symbols can be found on our website.

CH	Clubhouse	CG	Cattle Grid
PH	Public house	P	Post office
PC	Public convenience (in rural area)	MP	Milepost
TH	Town Hall, Guildhall or equivalent	MS	Milestone

ROCK FEATURES

Outcrop Cliff Scree

Tourist Information

Camp site / caravan site

Garden

Golf course or links

Information centre, all year / seasonal

Nature reserve

Parking / Park and ride, all year / seasonal

Picnic site

Selected places of tourist interest

Telephone, public / roadside assistance

Viewpoint

Visitor centre

Walks / Trails

Youth hostel

World Heritage site / area

Recreation / leisure / sports centre

ROADS AND PATHS

Not necessarily rights of way

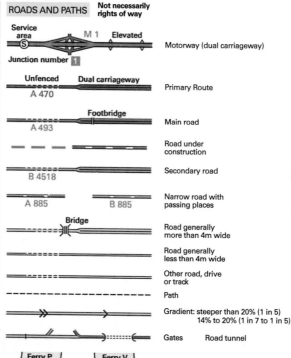

Motorway (dual carriageway)

Primary Route

Main road

Road under construction

Secondary road

Narrow road with passing places

Road generally more than 4m wide

Road generally less than 4m wide

Other road, drive or track

Path

Gradient: steeper than 20% (1 in 5)
14% to 20% (1 in 7 to 1 in 5)

Gates Road tunnel

Ferry (passenger) Ferry (vehicle)

RAILWAYS

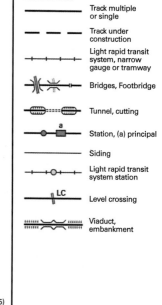

Track multiple or single

Track under construction

Light rapid transit system, narrow gauge or tramway

Bridges, Footbridge

Tunnel, cutting

Station, (a) principal

Siding

Light rapid transit system station

Level crossing

Viaduct, embankment

Map extract I: **Foinaven and Strath Dionard**
Landranger (1:50,000) Sheet 9: Cape Wrath

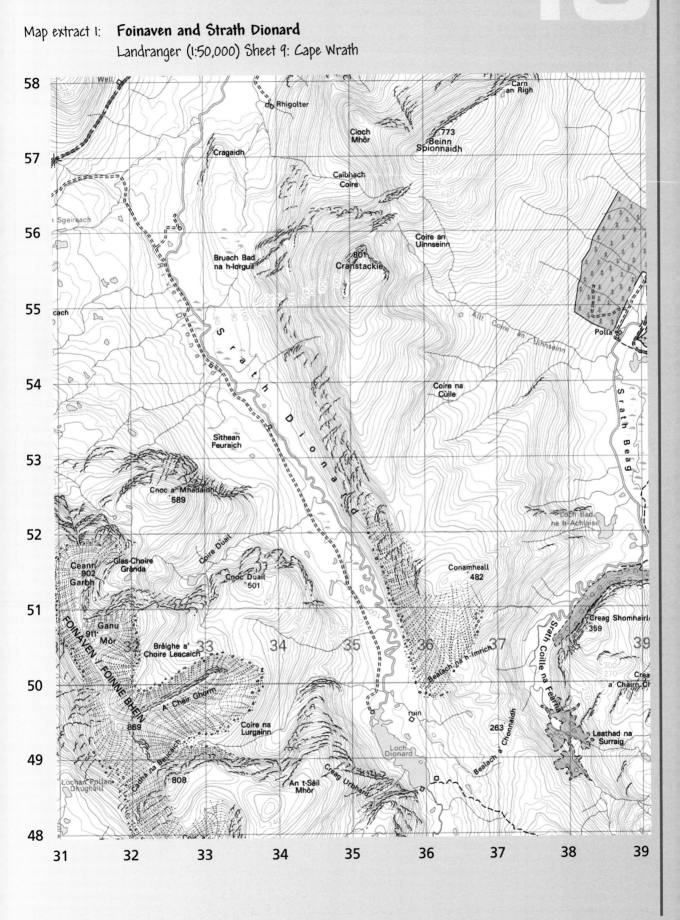

General question 1

(See Map extract 1)
Describe the physical features of the River Dionard and its valley between 354500 and 327560. **(4 KU marks)**

General answer 1

The River Dionard
flows in a north-westerly direction (✓). There are quite a few meanders (✓), for example in square 3551 (✓). There is an oxbow lake at 356506 (✓), and there are at least two tributaries joining in square 3354 (✓). The valley is U-shaped (✓), and there is marshy land on the flood plain in 3452 (✓).

Although there are five valid points in the first three sentences of this answer, markers would not award full marks until the last sentence, when the valley is mentioned. It is always good practice to give a grid reference, to show that you have correctly identified a feature.

Look out for

Give grid references when you are answering map questions. This allows statements you have made about places on the map to be checked to see whether you have read the map accurately. If you don't, you may lose out on a mark.

Look out for

In rivers questions, you are nearly always asked to describe the physical features of the river and its valley. You won't get full marks unless you do.

General question 2

Describe the various ways in which people could use the land shown on Map extract 1.

(4 ES marks)

General answer 2

The area could be used for lots of different outdoor activities (✓). For example, water sports could take place on Loch Dionard (✓) in square 3549 (✓). Many people will enjoy hillwalking on mountains such as Foinaven (3149) (✓) and even rock climbing (e.g. 333526) (✓). In winter, people could go cross-country skiing (✓).

The area might also be used for stalking and grouse shooting (✓).

It is important to use grid references where possible to show that you have read the map accurately. You will not receive a mark every time you use one, but it helps the examiners to see that you have identified something correctly. In this land-use question, it is helpful to indicate exactly where there are appropriate locations for most of the identified activities.

Credit question 1

Match these glacial features with the grid references (see Map extract 1). **(4 KU marks)**

319514	355490	375505	328500	344515
arête	truncated spur	ribbon loch	corrie	U-shaped valley

Although there are five features to identify, there are only four marks. This is because, if you get four correct, there will only be one reference left to choose from, which will also be correct. You must be very precise with your grid references and take time to look exactly at the point the six-figure reference refers to, not just the correct square.

Credit answer 1

Glacial feature	Grid reference
arête	328500
truncated spur	344515
ribbon loch	355490
corrie	319514
U-shaped valley	375505

Look out for

You will usually be expected to use six-figure grid references at Credit level, whereas four-figure grid references will often be enough at General level.

Credit question 2

Explain why most of the area shown on Map extract 1 is not suitable for commercial forestry.

(5 marks)

Credit answer 2

Most of the area shown is unsuitable for commercial forestry because the slopes are too steep for machinery to be able to plant or harvest the trees (✓).

There is only limited access to the area, with one track, several kilometres in length, making it difficult to transport timber (✓). There is a lot of bare rock in the area, such as the scree slopes in 3650 (✓), so it would be very difficult for trees to grow (✓). Much of the land is too high for trees to grow, as it would be cold, windy and exposed (✓). Soils on these high, steep slopes are likely to be thin and useless for growing trees (✓).

In this 'explain' question, it is vital to give reasons which show why the area is unsuitable for forestry. The first statement about the slopes being too steep only becomes a valid point when the answer explains that this makes it difficult to operate the machinery needed. In a question such as this, it is important to include explanations of how the physical factors (e.g. weather, slopes, soils) limit the possibilities for commercial forestry.

Urban map questions

What you should know at **General** and **Credit** level ...

Maps which are largely urban may test your knowledge on some physical Key Ideas such as river landscapes, but most of the questions will concentrate on human topics such as urban geography, industry, economic change and sometimes farming on the urban fringe.

You will be expected to know how to identify the different types of urban land-use zones on a map and to give evidence which backs up your choice of zone. You should be able to recognise the different street patterns which indicate old inner-city housing areas and also modern suburban housing (see diagram: Urban road patterns).

<u>Evidence that an area of map is the CBD:</u>

Main roads converging on the area, and sometimes an inner ring road; major transport terminals such as bus stations and railway stations; public services such as museums, art galleries and in particular tourist information offices and town halls; a large number of churches and/or a cathedral.

<u>Evidence that an area of map is the inner city:</u>

Grid-iron street patterns, indicating rows of terraced houses or, in Scotland, tenement buildings; buildings tightly packed, with little evidence of open space; evidence of industry among the residential areas and along old transport routes such as canals or railway lines.

<u>Evidence that an area of map is in the outer suburbs:</u>

Curvilinear street patterns with cul-de-sacs and crescents, indicating modern semi-detached and detached housing with gardens and driveways; more open space with evidence of parks, golf courses and school playing fields.

Diagram 16: <u>Urban road patterns</u>

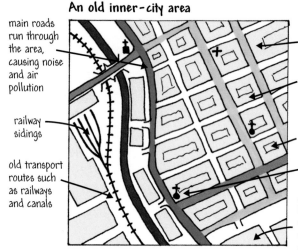

An old inner-city area

main roads run through the area, causing noise and air pollution

railway sidings

old transport routes such as railways and canals

grid-iron street pattern (rectilinear)

rows of terraced or tenement houses

little open space and few gardens

high number of churches

old industrial buildings close to housing and to old transport routes

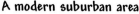

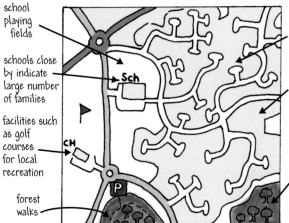

A modern suburban area

school playing fields

schools close by indicate large number of families

facilities such as golf courses for local recreation

forest walks

Sch

CH

P

curvilinear road pattern (many cul-de-sacs); few main roads

housing likely to be modern detached or semi-detached with large gardens and driveways

open land and wooded areas create a pleasant and attractive environment

!Look out for

Study the key to Ordnance Survey 1:50 000 maps on page 80 and familiarise yourself with the main symbols. This will save you time in the exam, even though there will be a key with the map in the exam.

Map extract 2: **Derby**

Landranger (1:50,000) Sheet 128: Derby

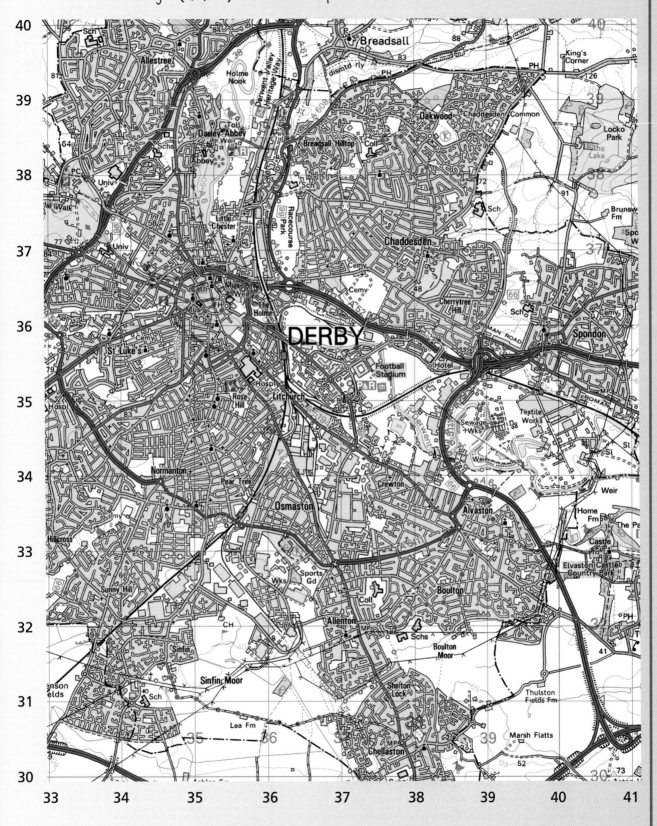

General question 1

(See Map extract 2)
Give map evidence to show that grid square 3536 contains the CBD (Central
Business District) of Derby.   **(4 ES marks)**

General answer 1

*This must contain Derby's CBD because there is a tourist information centre
(✓) and also two museums (✓). There is a bus station in the square (✓)
and also a cathedral (✓). Many main roads converge on this square (✓).*

Be precise when answering map questions. Many main roads
converging on an area in the middle of a town/city is evidence
that this zone could be the CBD. An area with one or more
main roads could be anywhere in the city or even in the
countryside! Don't be vague!

*There is other evidence
in this square that
Derby's CBD is located
here, but this answer
already gives plenty
of evidence to be able
to score full marks. It
is worth noting that,
in this particular map
question, there will be
no marks for giving a
grid reference, as the
question already states
that you must look in
grid square 3536.*

General question 2

(See Map extract 2)
Elvaston Castle Country Park is located in squares 4032 and 4033. What are the
advantages and disadvantages of this location for a Country Park?   **(4 ES marks)**

General answer 2

*There is a lake and a forest to attract wildlife (✓) and provide attractive
scenery (✓). There are also forest walks for people to go on (✓). It will be
easy for people to get there, as there is a main road (the A6) next to it (✓).
However, the road might also be a problem, as there will be noise and air
pollution (✓). Also, Home Farm is right next to the Country Park, and so
there might be problems with walkers on the farm's land (✓).*

Remember that each grid square is one kilometre across. This
is a quick way of estimating distance on OS maps, which could
help your answer in certain questions by stating, for example,
how close to a city a Country Park is located.

*To achieve full marks in
this answer, you must
give both advantages
and disadvantages. Note
that features such as
the A6 can be both an
advantage, by providing
good access, but also a
disadvantage by causing
pollution. You must
explain the benefits
and problems clearly,
as this answer does. It
is not sufficient to say
that it is a good location
for a Country Park
because it is next to the
A6. You must spell out
exactly how the A6 is
an advantage and/or a
problem.*

Credit question 1

(See Map extract 2)
Using map evidence, compare the residential environments of Normanton (3434) and Sinfin (3431). **(6 ES marks)**

Credit answer 1

Normanton is in the inner city, whereas Sinfin is in the outer suburbs (✓). The roads in Normanton are laid out mainly in a grid-iron pattern, whereas in Sinfin they are curvilinear (✓). As Sinfin is near the edge of the city, the land will be cheaper (✓), and so the houses will have gardens and driveways, whereas in Normanton the houses will be closely packed together with few gardens (✓), and cars will have to be parked mostly on the street, as there won't be space for driveways (✓). In Normanton, there will be old terraced housing, while in Sinfin the housing will be more modern (✓) and will be mainly detached or semi-detached (✓). The environment in Normanton might be quite polluted because it is close to the city centre, whereas at Sinfin the environment is likely to be cleaner and more attractive (✓), as there is open land and a golf course close by (✓).

Notice how, in this answer, each statement does not gain a mark until a clear comparison has been made. You must show how the areas are similar or different. It is usually best to do this in each sentence, rather than trying to describe the whole of one area first and then the second.

Credit question 2

(See Map extract 2)
There is a textile works in square 3934. Give the advantages and disadvantages of this site for manufacturing industry. **(6 ES marks)**

Credit answer 2

This is a good site for industry because there is flat land to build on (✓) and space around it to expand into (✓). There are excellent communications, as there are several main roads close by such as the A52 (✓), allowing easy access for workers and also for deliveries by lorry (✓). There is also a rail connection, allowing imports and exports by train (✓). There is a large workforce close by, as the site is in Derby (✓). However, there may be problems with this site, as it is on flat land next to the River Derwent and might flood (✓). It is right next to sewage works, so there could be unpleasant smells (✓). There may be problems with noise or air pollution from the factory, as there are housing areas just to the north and a Country Park just to the south (✓).

In this answer, you must show your knowledge of industrial location factors, by referring to evidence on the map. Always explain clearly why something you have identified is an advantage or disadvantage. For example, stating that this factory is on flat land will not get a mark until you explain that this is good because it is easy to build on or bad because it is next to the river and could flood.

Look out for

Learn how the different road types are shown on Ordnance Survey maps. **Motorways** are shown in blue and are labelled with the letter M (e.g. M6) on 1:50 000 maps. **Trunk** roads are shown in **green**, and **main** roads in **red**. They are both labelled with the letter A (e.g. A9).

Other types of map

What you should know at **General** and **Credit** level ...

Sometimes the Ordnance Survey map can be a mixture of urban and rural areas, such as Map 3 (Inverurie and Kintore). You will have to use your knowledge of different parts of the course and be prepared for some physical questions, say on rivers, and some urban questions, perhaps on site or function. There will often be a farming question on this type of map. The questions are no more difficult than on an urban or physical map, but there may simply be questions on a wider range of topics, so there are no additional skills that you need to learn to be able to answer these questions successfully.

General question 1

(See Map extract 3)
What is the main function of the town of Inverurie – a **tourist resort** or a **market town**? Give reasons for your answer.   **(4 ES marks)**

General answer 1

Inverurie is most likely to be a market town because there are many farms around it, such as Home Farm (7921) (✓), and farmers may bring their produce in to sell here (✓). Many roads lead into Inverurie, making it easy for farmers to access (✓). It is the largest town in the area shown by the map, so people will come into it from the countryside to use the town's services (✓). There are many services such as churches, schools and a railway station which are typical of a market town (✓).

General question 2

There are several areas of commercial forestry in the area shown on Map extract 3. What are the advantages of this area for commercial forestry?   **(4 ES marks)**

General answer 2

There is quite a lot of sloping land, for example in 7517 (✓), which is used for forestry because it is not so good for farm machinery (✓). There is a good network of roads in the area to transport timber (✓). There will be a workforce in Inverurie and Kintore (✓). The land is not too high, so the climate should be OK for growing trees (✓). It will not be too cold or too exposed (✓).

In this type of question, you must make a choice and use map evidence to support it. Inverurie could be either a tourist resort or a market town, so there is no mark for making the choice; you must gain all of the marks by finding relevant map evidence. Note that, as with many map questions, you will usually be given a mark for identifying a relevant feature on the map, as the question does not specify a particular grid reference. It is always worth showing that you can read the map accurately.

This answer gains marks for identifying factors which show that the map area is favourable for growing trees. Often, this will be to do with climatic factors, relief of the land and accessibility. This answer also gains a mark for identifying a relevant grid reference.

Map extract 3: **Inverurie and Kintore**
Landranger (1:50,000) Sheet 38: Aberdeen

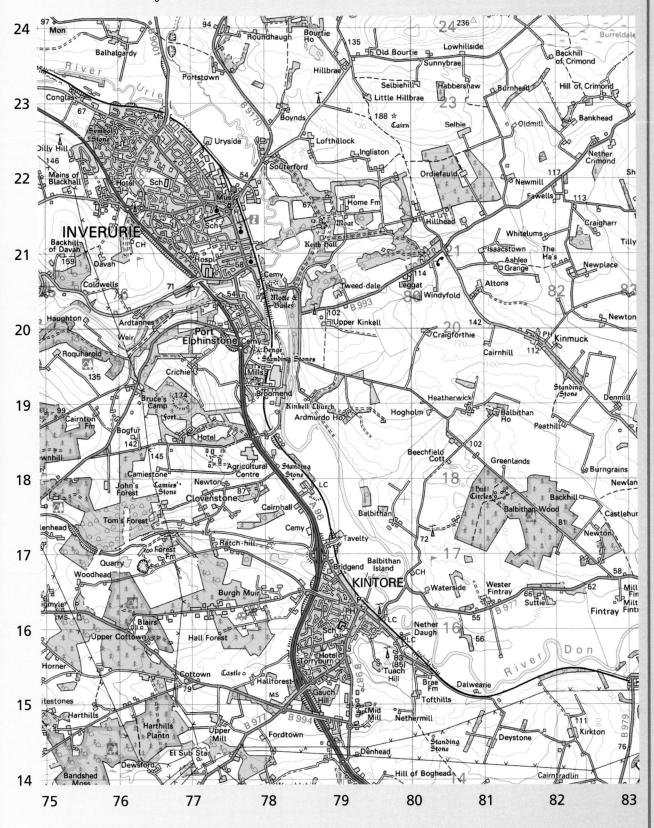

Credit question 1

(See Map extract 3)
Describe the physical features of the River Don **and** its valley between 783193 and 830159. **(4 KU marks)**

Credit answer 1

At 783193, there is an island in the river (✓). The River Don flows mainly in a south-easterly direction (✓) until 810152, where it changes to a mainly easterly direction (✓). There is an oxbow lake at 799160 (✓), and the flood plain is about 1 kilometre wide in squares 8215 and 8216 (✓). It is not a particularly deep valley and has many large meanders (✓), so the River Don is likely to be in its lower course here (✓).

To achieve full marks, you must describe the river and its valley. This answer refers to the flood plain, which counts as a valley feature. So, because of this and the other valid points, this answer is able to achieve full marks.

Credit question 2

Find Brae Farm at 802153 on Map extract 3.

'This is an excellent location for farming.'

Do you agree fully with this statement? Give reasons for your answer. **(6 ES marks)**

Credit answer 2

I do not fully agree with this statement, as there are some problems for the farm. A railway runs through the farmland, and this might cause inconvenience for the farmworkers trying to get to land on the other side (✓). Land close to the River Don is flat and might flood (✓), although the soil is likely to be fertile because of alluvial deposits (✓). There are electricity pylons, which could be difficult for farm machinery to work around (✓). However, there is a lot of gently sloping land which is easy for machinery to work on, so this would make it a good location for arable farming (✓). Also, it is close to Kintore and Inverurie, from where workers could be hired (✓), and there is good access to the A96 dual carriageway, so produce could be taken to market quickly (✓).

This question is deliberately phrased to encourage you to say that you only partially agree. This way, you can give both good and bad points about the location of the farm, which will make it easier to pick up marks. You can still fully agree or disagree, but then you will have to find six points in favour of, or disagreeing with, the statement. Always refer to map evidence to show that you have studied the map closely. This answer does so by referring to the names of the nearby settlements and the number of the dual carriageway (A96). Make sure that you state why being close to a main road is good (or bad).

Look out for

You may partially agree and partially disagree with a statement, so long as you give valid reasons for and against it. Often, this may enable you to gain marks more easily.

Glossary

abrasion   erosion caused by the scraping and scouring action of rock fragments carried by glaciers (or rivers, or waves)

accessibility   how easy a place is to get to

air mass   a large body of air with specific characteristics which affects the weather when it arrives in an area

alluvium   fertile material left behind after a river floods (also called silt)

alternative energy   renewable energy sources such as wind, wave or solar power which are clean and do not pollute the environment in the way that fossil fuels do

altitude   height of a place above sea level

anemometer   instrument which records wind speed

anticyclone   an area of high pressure (usually brings fine, dry weather)

arable farming   growing crops

Arctic maritime   air mass originating in the Arctic bringing very cold weather and snow in winter

arête   a narrow, knife-edged ridge, formed by glacial erosion

aspect   the direction in which a slope or settlement faces

balance of trade   the difference between the values of a country's imports and exports

barograph   instrument used for measuring air pressure

bilateral aid   help given to a country by another country (usually with strings attached)

birth rate   the number of live births per 1000 people per year

boulder clay   a mixture of glacial moraine, rocks and rock fragments

brownfield site   land in an urban area which has been previously built on and is awaiting redevelopment

canopy   dense tree foliage high up off the ground blocking out sunlight to the areas below

catchment area   the land from which a river and its tributaries gather their water; also referred to as the drainage basin

census   national population survey carried out to gather information about the population in a country

central business district   the commercial and business centre of a town, where land values are highest

charitable aid   aid given by charities, where money has been donated by people

cirque   corrie (used in England and North America)

cold front   the boundary between cold and warm air where air is rapidly forced upwards, creating cumulonimbus clouds, often giving short heavy downpours

commuter   someone who travels some distance to and from their work each day

confluence   the point where two rivers join

congestion   when road traffic is so heavy that jams occur and journey times are lengthened

conservation   the protection of resources and the environment from harm

contour   line drawn on a map joining points of equal height above sea level

conurbation   a large city which has spread outwards and joined up with other towns in the area (e.g. Clydeside, or Greater Manchester)

corrasion   erosion caused by the scraping and scouring effect of material carried by rivers (or glaciers, or waves)

corrie   a deep rounded hollow with steep slopes carved out of a mountain by glacial erosion

corrie lochan   a lake in the saucer-shaped hollow at the bottom of a corrie

counter-urbanisation   when people move out of cities to get away from the problems associated with them such as pollution and congestion

crop rotation   when different crops are planted in a field in successive years to help maintain soil fertility

cul-de-sac   a road which stops and doesn't lead anywhere else

cumulonimbus   towering clouds which often bring heavy downpours and sometimes electrical storms

cumulus   clouds with a fluffy appearance formed due to condensation caused by convection currents

curvilinear   pattern of roads consisting of many crescents and cul-de-sacs, used in modern housing areas to create safer residential environments

cwm   corrie (used in Wales)

death rate   the number of deaths per 1000 people per year

deforestation   the total clearance of forested land

delta   deposits found at the mouth of a river (often forming islands)

demographic transition model   a model showing how birth and death rates change over time

densely populated   an area with a lot of people per square kilometre

deposition   when material is left behind by rivers, ice or the sea

depression   an area of low pressure associated with active weather fronts

desertification   when land gradually turns into desert

developed country   usually quite a wealthy country with a high standard of living and good services; also known as economically more developed countries (EMDCs)

developing country   usually quite a poor country with a low standard of living and a lack of services; also known as economically less developed countries (ELDCs)

dormitory settlement   a place where a lot of people live but have to travel to work somewhere else

drainage basin   the land drained by a river and its tributaries; also referred to as the catchment area

drought   prolonged period of dry weather

eastings   the numbered grid lines along the bottom and top of the map, getting higher towards the east

ELDC   economically less developed country; also known as a developing country

Glossary

EMDC economically more developed country; also known as a developed country

emergency aid aid given quickly following a major disaster such as an earthquake

environment the surroundings in which people, plants and animals live

erosion the wearing away of land caused by moving ice, rivers or waves

erratic large boulder which has been transported and deposited by ice in an area where it is out of place

explain give reasons for

exploitation the selfish use of resources or people for economic gain without regard for the human or environmental consequences

exports goods and services sold to other countries

eyot an island formed by deposition in a river channel

fair trade trade where the producers (usually in developing countries) get a fair price for their goods

farm diversification when farms branch out into new ways of getting income, apart from traditional food production

firn hard compacted snow; the stage between freshly fallen snow and the formation of glacial ice

flood plain area of flat land on either side of a river which is flooded when the river bursts its banks

fodder crops grown to feed to livestock

fossil fuels energy resources such as coal, oil and natural gas formed from the fossilised remains of plants and animals

frost shattering a type of weathering where rock is broken up by repeated freezing and thawing of water contained in small cracks (also known as freeze–thaw)

function the main purpose of a town or city; settlements often have several different functions such as port, market town, administrative centre

gathering techniques ways in which information can be collected about a given area; refers to fieldwork methods

glacier very slow-moving mass of ice flowing from corries down a valley

global warming the gradual rise in world temperatures thought to be due to the increase in levels of carbon dioxide and other gases due to human activities

grant money given to an industry such as farming, by the government or the EU, to help its development

greenbelt land around the edge of a city where building is severely restricted in order to protect the countryside and stop the outward spread of built-up areas

greenfield site land which has never been built on before, often at the edge of a town or city

grid-iron parallel pattern of roads intersected at right angles by another series of parallel roads; often found in old inner-city areas; can be referred to as rectilinear

hanging valley small U-shaped valley left high above a larger U-shaped valley formed by a tributary glacier which could not erode down as far as the glacier in the main valley

heavy industry factories producing manufactured goods which require large amounts of heavyweight raw materials, e.g. shipbuilding, steelmaking

HEP hydro-electric power: electricity generated by the force of water falling on to turbines

high-order service shop or facility where expensive products are sold but purchased only occasionally by each individual

hot desert hot dry areas, usually found close to the tropics, which have less than 250 millimetres of rainfall per year

hydraulic action type of erosion caused by the sheer force of water breaking off material from the bed or banks of a river or from the coastline

ice plucking where ice at the bottom of a glacier freezes on to weathered rock and pulls it away as the glacier moves forward

immigrant a person arriving in a country to live or work

imports goods and services bought by a country from abroad

industrial estate a group of factories in a specially built development, designed to give them all the services and space they need

infant mortality the number of deaths of children under one year old per 1000 live births

inner city land-use zone immediately beyond the CBD, where factories and workers' houses were built during the industrial revolution

interlocking spurs hill slopes projecting into a V-shaped valley, between which a river meanders

isobar line on a synoptic chart joining points of equal air pressure

land-use conflict disagreement over how an area of land should be used

lateral moraine rock debris deposited at the side of a glacier, often along the length of a valley

leaching the process by which minerals and nutrients are washed out of the soil due to large amounts of rainfall.

life expectancy the average number of years that a person born in a particular country is expected to live for

light industry factories producing goods with a high value-to-weight ratio, e.g. computers, electrical equipment

literacy rate the proportion of people who can read and write

long-term aid help given to a country over many years, often for major projects such as HEP schemes and road-building

low-order service shop or facility where low-cost products are sold and which are purchased frequently by each individual

market town town surrounded by a large number of farms where agricultural products are brought to be sold

meander a bend in a river

medial moraine line of rock debris down the centre of a valley created by the lateral moraines of two tributary glaciers joining together

medium-order service shop or facility where medium-cost products are sold which are purchased quite often by each individual

migration movement of people from one place to another to live or work

millibars units of measurement for air pressure

millimetres one tenth of a centimetre: units of measurement for precipitation

mixed farming where both crops and animals are produced on a farm

moraine material deposited by a glacier

mouth the point where a river flows into the sea

multilateral aid aid given by large organisations, such as the United Nations or World Bank, which are funded by many different countries

muskeg boggy land found during the summer in tundra areas where melted snow cannot drain away because of permafrost

National Park a large area of attractive scenery which is protected from harmful developments so that people living in and visiting the area can enjoy a relatively unspoilt environment

natural increase how fast a country's population is increasing, calculated by finding the difference between a country's birth and death rate; often referred to as population growth rate

névé hard compacted snow; the stage between freshly fallen snow and the formation of glacial ice

northings the numbered grid lines up the sides of the map, getting higher towards the north

occluded front where warm and cold fronts have met, often causing bad weather

okta a measurement of cloud cover representing one eighth of the visible sky

outwash plain area beyond the snout of a glacier which is covered in meltwater deposits

overcultivation where soil becomes exhausted due to farming activities which cannot be sustained; one of the causes of desertification

overfishing where fish stocks become low and may be threatened with extinction because too many fish are being caught

overgrazing where livestock are allowed to graze on marginal land for too long, resulting in vegetation being destroyed; one of the causes of desertification

overpopulation where the resources of an area can no longer support the number of people living there; one of the causes of desertification

oxbow lake an abandoned meander which is crescent-shaped and now separate from the main river channel

pastoral farming which involves only the rearing of animals (e.g. sheep)

pedestrianisation where traffic is banned from a street to create a safer and more pleasant environment for shoppers

permafrost permanently frozen sub-soil found in tundra areas

polar continental air mass originating over land areas in northern Europe, bringing bitterly cold weather

polar maritime air mass originating in northerly sea areas, bringing cold wet weather

pollution contamination of the environment by noise, dirt, fumes or other harmful substances due to human activities

population density the average number of people living in each square kilometre of an area

population growth rate how fast a country's population is increasing, calculated by finding the difference between a country's birth and death rate; often referred to as natural increase

population pyramid a graph showing the proportion of males and females in each age group for an area or country

population structure how a population is made up according to gender and age

precipitation different types of moisture, coming mainly from clouds, landing on the ground; includes rain, snow, sleet, hail and drizzle

prevailing wind the most common wind direction in a particular area

primary industry industry which extracts raw materials from the land or sea; includes farming, fishing, mining, quarrying, etc.

processing techniques methods used to display information; includes bar charts, pie charts, tables, line graphs, etc.

pull factors things which might attract people to an area, e.g. better standard of living, higher pay

push factors things which might make people want to leave an area, e.g. lack of jobs, drought

pyramidal peak a jagged or pointed mountain which has been affected by the formation of corries on three or more sides

quality of life a measure of how comfortable and content people are with their lives

quotas where a limit has been imposed on a commodity, e.g. on the production of milk or on the number of fish caught

rain gauge instrument used to measure precipitation

range of temperature the difference between the highest and lowest average temperatures

raw materials natural resources used to make other products

rectilinear parallel pattern of roads intersected at right angles by another series of parallel roads; often found in old inner-city areas; can be referred to as grid-iron

refugee someone who has been displaced from their home area by war, persecution or a natural disaster

relief the shape and height of the land

renewable resource a resource such as wave, wind or hydro-electric power which can be used over and over again without it ever running out

ribbon loch a long narrow loch formed in a U-shaped valley due to glacial erosion

river beach beach on the inside of a meander formed by the deposition of river material

river braiding where a river deposits material in the middle of its channel, creating islands and causing it to split temporarily into different channels

river cliff vertical or overhanging slope on the outside of a meander, caused by river erosion

route centre a settlement where many different roads (or railways) meet; this might have been one of the reasons for its growth

rural to do with the countryside

STANDARD GRADE GEOGRAPHY

rural–urban fringe land at the very edge of the city where the built-up area meets the countryside

rural–urban migration movement of people from the countryside to the city, usually in an attempt to improve their standard of living

science park a type of industrial estate where the main companies involved are high-technology research and design activities, e.g. biotechnology

secondary industry industry which manufactures goods using a variety of raw materials

self-help scheme a project, usually in a developing country where, for a small amount of money, local people are able to learn new skills and help their own communities in a variety of different ways

set-aside land land which is left uncultivated and for which the farmer receives a government grant

settlement a place where people live

shanty town a ramshackle group of houses, often at the edge of developing-world cities, which the inhabitants have built themselves using whatever materials they can get hold of

shifting cultivation type of farming carried out by indigenous people in the tropical rainforests, where farming activities move on to new ground every few years due to poor soil fertility

short-term aid aid given, usually to developing countries, which is intended to help out immediately following a crisis such as an earthquake; can include tents, blankets, clean water, medical supplies, etc.; often known also as emergency aid

silt fertile material left behind after a river floods (also called alluvium)

site the land on which a settlement is built

situation where a settlement is in relation to other places in that area; also called location

snout the front end of a glacier; sometimes referred to as the toe

source the point (usually in the hills) where a river begins

sparsely populated an area with very few people per square kilometre

sphere of influence the area around a settlement or service from which it draws shoppers/customers

standard of living how well off a person or population is

Stevenson screen white box at a weather station containing instruments for measuring temperature and humidity

stratus low layer of cloud, often found close to the warm front

striations scratches left on flat rock which have been caused by rocks frozen into the base of an ice sheet or glacier, abrading the bedrock as the ice moved along

suburbs the outlying districts of a city, made up mainly of housing areas

sustainable something which can be maintained indefinitely without damaging the environment or depleting resources for future generations

synoptic chart weather map using symbols for fronts, isobars and different weather stations

tariff a tax, imposed selectively on goods being brought into a country, which is designed to protect local producers of the same product

terminal moraine mound of rock debris deposited by a glacier at its snout

tertiary industry industry providing services to other people (e.g. transport, medical and retail services)

tied aid type of bilateral aid given to a country by another country where conditions apply to the country receiving the aid; for example, the aid may be in the form of a loan which has to be paid back with interest

tourist resort a town or place which caters for large number of tourists

trade the movement of goods and services between countries

trade alliance a group of countries which have joined together to give themselves more economic power in world trade, e.g. the European Union

trade deficit where the value of a country's imports exceeds the value of its exports, resulting in an overall loss

trade surplus where the value of a country's exports exceeds the value of its imports, resulting in an overall profit

transportation the movement of material by rivers, ice or the sea

tributary a small river which joins a larger one

tropical continental air mass originating from land near the tropics, bringing warm dry weather

tropical hardwood timber taken from tropical rainforests such as teak, ebony, mahogany and rosewood

tropical maritime air mass originating from sea areas over the tropics, bringing warm wet weather

truncated spur a slope on a hillside which originally extended further into a valley but which has had its end sliced off by a glacier

tundra cold desert areas found in extreme northern latitudes

urban to do with built-up areas such as towns and cities

urbanisation the increase in the proportion of people living in towns and cities

U-shaped valley a valley with steep sides and a flat bottom which has been carved by a glacier, giving the valley a U-shaped cross-sectional profile

voluntary aid aid given by charitable organisations, such as Oxfam and the Red Cross, which are funded by donations mainly from the public; also known as charitable aid

V-shaped valley a valley with steep sides and a narrow bottom which has been carved by a river, usually in its upper course, giving the valley a V-shaped cross-sectional profile

warm front boundary between cold and warm air where the warm air rises slowly up over the cold air, causing the formation of stratus and cumulus clouds giving a prolonged spell of rain

weather front boundary between air masses of different temperatures

weathering the breakdown of rocks by physical and chemical processes caused by the weather

wind vane instrument used to indicate the direction from which the wind is blowing